STARTING FROM
scratch

STARTING FROM
scratch

[
SECRETS FROM 21 ORDINARY
PEOPLE WHO MADE THE
ENTREPRENEURIAL LEAP
]

WES MOSS

Dearborn™
Trade Publishing
A **Kaplan Professional** Company

This publication is designed to provide accurate and authoritative information in regard to the subject matter covered. It is sold with the understanding that the publisher is not engaged in rendering legal, accounting, or other professional service. If legal advice or other expert assistance is required, the services of a competent professional person should be sought.

President, Dearborn Publishing: Roy Lipner
Vice President and Publisher: Cynthia A. Zigmund
Senior Acquisitions Editor: Michael Cunningham
Development Editor: Karen Murphy
Interior Design: Lucy Jenkins
Cover Design: Jody Billert/Design Literate
Typesetting: Todd Bowman

Printed in the United States of America

05 06 07 10 9 8 7 6 5 4 3 2

Library of Congress Cataloging-in-Publication Data

Moss, Wes.
    Starting from scratch : secrets from 21 ordinary people who made the entrepreneurial leap / Wes Moss.
        p. cm.
    ISBN 1-4195-2106-3 (6x9 hardcover)
    1. Businesspeople–United States–Biography. 2. Entrepreneurship–United States–Biography. 3. Success in business–United States. I. Title.
    HC102.5.A2M67 2005
    338'.04'092273–dc22

                                                          2005019395

Contents

Acknowledgments

Having undertaken the writing of a book for the first time, it's a small miracle that you are reading it at all, that my business is still growing, and that my wife hasn't killed me yet. This project was similar to starting my own second company, and as I explain later in the book, no successful venture is ever achieved by the efforts of one person alone. So in the spirit of giving credit where credit is due, I would like to thank the following groups of people:

■ My Family

- Primarily, the burden of completing a book like this rests on the shoulders of the family who tolerates you during the writing process. My wife Lynne patiently supported me and acted as my primary focus group throughout this entire project. She deserves the credit for keeping me on track, and for making sure my stories were relatable and understandable.

- My parents, the veterinarian John and the real estate agent Claudia, preached the value of independence and entrepreneurship as long as my siblings Brannan, Kip, Lilly, and I can remember.

Business Associates

- My business partners, Dan, Tim, and Steve, are patient and supportive of all of my endeavors, and a true entrepreneur, Jerry Johnson, continues to lead with his word.
- All of my current clients continue to educate me by sharing the intimate details of their own entrepreneurial stories—specifically, the remarkable Linda B., the exceptional William K., and the extraordinary Ned and Barbara P., who put their trust in me and taught me the truest measure of business.

My Friends

- My oldest friends from Chapel Hill deserve their own stories, though more a screenplay than business nonfiction. Their influence and encouragement are immeasurable. So thank you Scott, Jason, Tony, Kevin, and Troy for all of your help.
- Andy Litinsky, my genius young friend, thank you for your enthusiasm, entrepreneurial spirit, and brilliant ideas along the way.
- On the development, organization, and production of *Starting from Scratch*, thank you to my good friends Judy and G.G., who were with me from the start; to Libby and Camille, who were on board since day one tracking down some of my most interesting stories; and to all of the wonderful people I interviewed and whose stories were not included.
- Thank you to all of the people who, like me, tend to underestimate their obstacles and who advised me to push forward

with the project; thank you Lew Dickey and Barbara Babbitt Kaufman.

- Thank you wholeheartedly to all of the people who told me the book could never be done, and to the naysayers who said the idea would never get off the ground. There's nothing more motivating than someone insisting "It can't be done."

■ Interviewees

- The entrepreneurs who I interviewed for this book, now friends after the time we spent together, dug deep and shared their intriguing stories and most sincere business advice and secrets. I can't wait to see what the future holds for this magnificent crew of people.

■ My Publisher

- And finally, the remarkable group at Dearborn Trade Publishing who understood my vision from day one. From the very beginning of the project, I knew I had found a group of people who believed in me more. From Marketing and PR to the security blanket of my editor, thank you all for adding value and for being on board.

Introduction

Do you ever get a sick feeling in your gut on Sunday night knowing that Monday morning you have to go to a humdrum job working for someone else? You've got the Sunday night blues. So did all 21 people in this book.

The stories you are about to read are those of ordinary people just like yourself who got tired of dreading the beginning of each week. They made that sick feeling go away by building wealth and security doing what they love. How? By starting their own companies—from scratch. It wasn't always easy. But these 21 people share the very secrets that guided and helped them along the way. Their stories can empower you to get out of the paycheck rut, build your own wealth and security through entrepreneurship, and find a career you actually love.

If you have ever wanted to work for yourself but could never figure out which career path to choose, then this is the right book for you. I've done the research for you. I've traveled all over the country—to more than 16 different cities—and interviewed dozens of ordinary people who became extraordinary entrepreneurs. Just read their stories, listen to their secrets, and think about how you would fit into one of their industries. This is the final step you have been waiting for, the step that will finally lead you toward a life where you are living to work and not working to live.

Even if you're willing to put up with a boring job in exchange for security, you're not as secure as you think. That security, which is the main reason most people go to work for a large organization—is largely an illusion based on the way things were 50 years ago. Look at the headlines about corporations dumping pension plans and corporate scandals that wipe out the life savings of their employees. And look at all the 50-somethings getting laid off because their salaries are too expensive for the company, which can pay less to younger employees. Gradually, our American economy is rewarding people less and less for being loyal to corporate bosses.

Why should you listen to me? Because I know the kind of people who find financial security in today's economy. In my work as a financial advisor, I meet them all the time. They fit into two main groups. The first group is what I call the "lottery" group: They happened to work for a stellar, top-tier, upper 1 percent company such as Home Depot, Microsoft, or UPS and got in early, riding the company to the top. Or they inherited money. Or they hit it big with one great idea that turned into a public company and made them millions. This book is not about that lucky group of people—your chances of working for the next Microsoft are less than your chances of winning the lottery. This book is about the second group of financially secure people: the entrepreneurs. They're people who methodically build up wealth through doing what they love and working hard at it. This book is about those average people who start and build a successful business.

Here's why starting your own business is so important now: there's been a huge shift in the way the world works. My grandparents were trained to be taken care of by some sort of corporate job; they were *not* taught to do what they love. I just heard an 86-year-old stand up at a Rotary Club meeting and tell the story of how he got his first job. It's the same way a lot of people used to find work. His father went to one of his friends and said, "Can my boy work for you?" The standard protocol was that if the friend gave your son a job, your son had to work at the job for at least 3 years before he even thought about moving anywhere else. If he did leave after 3 years, and that was frowned on, there was an unwritten rule that he would never work for the competition. Could you imagine that today? This particular man worked at the same company for 42 years. My grandfather worked at DuPont for 30 years and retired with a nice chunk of DuPont stock and a nice pension, which allowed him to fully retire for the rest of his life. And for that generation, retirement wasn't that long—they only expected to live to their mid-70s.

Look how things have changed. Generation Y could literally stand for "Why stay at any job for more than a year?" It's not because we're different from our grandparents. It's because our generation has seen our parents' generation embrace the same story their parents believed in: pensions, corporate bonuses, the belief that the company would take care of them for life. My parents' generation had to find ways to play catch-up instead. They earned professional degrees and opened their own practices. They had to figure out ways to save more and be more creative.

Still, today our number one fear is outliving our money. To retire with $60,000 to $80,000 in investment income annually, you may need well over a million dollars. That's something to keep you awake at night. Saving that kind of money on today's paychecks seems nearly impossible. But building your own business into a valuable asset *is* doable. People are realizing this and starting their own businesses in record numbers. They don't want to learn the hard way that corporate America may not provide for them. More and more people are finding the best person to work for is themselves. And the best way to do that is to do something they love, something they know they can do for a long time because they enjoy it.

People want to know how to build security and work at something meaningful. That's why reality shows like *The Apprentice* are so popular: people want to get out of their ordinary lives and see the fascinating ways that others make a living. Their stories take us out of our dissatisfying jobs for a moment and put us into something different. After the show, they dismiss their fascination with business start-ups by muttering, "The grass always looks greener on the other side."

I'm telling you that sometimes the grass really is greener. People who build their own businesses really *are* more fulfilled—and often more financially secure—because they do what they're good at. And as they go along, they keep getting better. Every day challenges them to rise to the occasion in a perpetual cycle of self-improvement. I always ask myself these questions: What am I doing with my life? What do I do for a living, and why? If you don't have a good answer to these questions, and if you aren't proud to talk about what you do for a livelihood, then *Starting from Scratch* will help you find the answers. I've spent my career listening to people who hate what they do and people who love what they do. The ones who love what they do are living the American dream and living a bountiful, exciting, and fulfilling life. The ones who hate what they do end up living a life of misery. This book focuses on helping you land in the first camp.

As I heard the stories of entrepreneurs—regular entrepreneurs, not billionaires—I noticed a rhythm to their stories. A four-step mode of operation that has led them all toward extreme entrepreneurial success. These steps are remarkably easy to remember, and easy to implement. I call these steps the HUNT.

I promise you, if you can master the four steps that I outline in what I call the art of the HUNT, and listen to the secrets from these 21 stories, then you will be well on your way to achieving an entrepreneurial mind-set and realizing extraordinary success.

The HUNT works like this:

- **Harness what you have.** Embark on an internal, two-part process of self-discovery. First, identify your inherent skills. Second, figure out something tangible that you love: a product, industry, or trade you are proud to be associated with. Put them together and you've got a business venture.

- **Underestimate your obstacles.** Practice the learned trait of optimism. Define a vision and mentally bypass the multitude of things that can go wrong or stand in your way so you can focus on your own personal and all-important vision.
- **Notice your network.** Engage in a process of external recognition. Find those around you who can assist you in realizing your vision, and utilize the leverage that others provide in reaching your particular goal.
- **Take the first step.** Develop a bias toward action. This step provides the catalyst that makes any entrepreneurial dream or vision turn into reality. Without it, there is no HUNT.

It's human nature to hunt; it always has been. Our methods have changed over time, but we are still hunting for opportunities in order to feed and shelter ourselves and our families. Instead of using clubs, spears, bows, or guns, the entrepreneurial mind-set uses the Internet and marketing plans. And rather than looking for a warmer, dryer cave, we're now looking for a bigger home, a more substantial retirement fund, and more vacation time. The entrepreneurial mind-set comes from the basic human need for self-preservation.

For example, when I was a teenager growing up in rural Pennsylvania, I *harnessed* what I had—lots of open space, a good reputation with my younger siblings' friends, and a whole summer with nothing to do. I harnessed all that and set up a day camp in my parent's house. Of course, there were obstacles, but I *underestimated* them: I didn't have a car, so I'd have the kids come to me. I'd never been a camp counselor, but I figured it was like playing with my little brothers and sister. I didn't want to serve meals, but I could have the kids bring brown bag lunches. Also, I *noticed my network*: my little brother became my only employee; my parents became helpers by buying snacks like juice and crackers; and my neighbors would become customers. Finally, I *took the first step* and mailed out questionnaires to 50 families asking questions about the kinds of activities and times that would appeal to them. After that, I kept on using that cycle to set up my camp and operate it three days a week. That summer when I was 14 years old, I made $3,000 a month for three days of work each week. Whether through a lemonade stand or a lawn-mowing business, most of us play at the game of earning money as a child.

If you look back on your life, you can probably see the HUNT principles at work. Whether it was a money-earning project or just a hobby, you have talents that you have harnessed to accomplish things. But then, somewhere along the way you got the idea that this wasn't really work. You stopped taking yourself seriously and started trying to fit into what other people thought you should do, what would be prestigious, or what was considered safe. That's the kind of thinking that squeezes the will to hunt out of people. But you can get it back.

Instead of explaining the steps of the HUNT myself, I'm going to use the stories of 21 successful entrepreneurs to explain how it works. All of the ordinary people in these stories demonstrate the four principles of the HUNT. And if you look at people around you and at your own life, it will become apparent how you have instinctually used these principles in parts of your life.

We only have so much time in the day, so we can either enjoy our journey through life or work at something we hate and try to squeeze everything else into what little free time is left. My message is that this world would be a much better place if people worked at what they loved. If you're not doing it now, get inspired by people who are. Learn how to HUNT in the 21st century and let the HUNT help you *start from scratch*.

Harness What You Have

The first part of the HUNT, the H, has to do with harnessing your skills, which usually involves the things you love. If you think making money doing what you love is impossible, it's no wonder—our whole education system is geared toward training people to fit into a larger organization. Imagine what it would be like if you focused on what you're good at and figured out how you could make a living from that and contribute to the world around you.

First off, identify your natural edge. For instance, in Part One you'll read about people who found their edge. Warren Brown and Ian Gerard both have a skill for inspiring people of all walks of life to take up their cause; Maria Churchill and Connie Grunwaldt have a natural edge for selling; Dave Helfrick is a natural-born dealmaker; and Dany Levy is a gifted writer. They are all good at other things, but in these areas they are exceptional.

The next part of the H is external: figure out your natural draw. Find out the product, trade, or industry for which you have a passion. You need to search for an economically viable area to apply your strengths; finding this area is key. Ask yourself, What product, industry, or trade fascinates me? Take time to remember the things you loved as a child and think about what you wanted to be when you grew up. What section of the bookstore is your first destination? What section of the newspaper do you read first? Do you read arts and leisure, or do you go right to the real estate section? Don't discount these natural draws.

Then, put the two parts of the H together: the natural edge with the natural draw. You need both parts to make the H step complete. Finding both parts of the H step can take days, months, or even years. This process of self-discovery is the biggest challenge. You need to be patient with it and realize that you'll figure it out over time as long as you focus on it. Eventually, you'll figure out your natural edge and your natural draw. Finally, put the two together and you'll complete the first step of the HUNT.

Having trouble harnessing what you have? Check out the stories of these first six ordinary people. Their secrets embody six different approaches to harnessing what you have:

- **Find the love.** Maria Churchill was left empty by the corporate jobs she had been steered toward all her life. It wasn't until the dot-com bubble burst—and she went through three layoffs—that she started searching for her natural edge through self-help books, career counseling, and even a shamanic journey.
- **Desperately seeking challenge.** No matter what she did, Dany Levy's thirst for learning and challenge in her writing career was frustrated by her jobs in New York's magazine industry. By pushing herself to keep on learning, she came up with something new.
- **Confidence.** Dave Helfrich was good at making deals and he knew it. But his corporate job wasn't going to reward him for this skill. Instead of putting up with it, he made a bold move that most of his

friends and family thought was foolish. It turned out to be a genius of an idea.

- **Common vision.** Ian Gerard combined his natural edge for engaging others with his natural draw toward culture. He created a not-for-profit organization that answered a need in the nation's art communities.
- **Decisive progression.** Connie Grunwaldt developed her natural edge for selling over more than a decade in corporate America. After years of picking up the real estate section of the newspaper first, she discovered her natural draw to the housing industry and took the Chicago real estate market by storm.
- **Have a cause.** Warren Brown was driven by causes but was getting beaten down by his career in the public sector. He found a new cause in the lucrative natural foods industry.

Let yourself dream about how you could take one of these business models and make it your own. Instead of selling European shoes like Maria Churchill, why not cigars or private-label Scotch? Whatever you choose to do, it starts with dreaming about the possibilities. As you read, let your imagination run wild and dream up your own way to harness what you have. Let the HUNT begin.

■ Chapter One

Maria Churchill, Founder of **Debout Shoes**

Find the Love

After nearly 15 humdrum years hawking goods for corporate America, Maria Churchill finally loves what she does—and the answer was at her feet all along.

Maria's story begins in corporate America, complete with a nice corporate salary plus expense account, and ends up in a shoe boutique on Los Angeles's Ventura Boulevard. Now that she's owner of Debout Shoe and Deboutshoes.com, Maria is finally spending her days doing what she loves. It's been a long road. She's living proof that you can turn your love into your business.

The fantasy of corporate America appealed to Maria early. From the time she was a girl, she'd had the idea that climbing the corporate ladder was her "ticket to making money and anything I wanted in life." Says Maria, "All the voices around me, from my parents to teachers and society, were all about security and going to work for a big corporation. That's what people did in the '80s." After college, when she was recruited by a major printer manufacturer to work in procurement, Maria figured she was living her dream.

When she talks about those early days, Maria laughs at how obvious it should have been: she just didn't love it the way she thought she would. Even though everyone else was impressed with her big title and nice office, Maria was a round peg trying to fit into a square hole. At the time, it wasn't clear at all. First, she thought she didn't like working in procurement, so she switched to sales at IBM. Then, she thought she didn't like the technology industry, so she switched to clothing and worked at the Levi Strauss & Co. Everyone around her was dazzled by her successes. But in her private moments, she would look up at her coworkers and think, *They are all like a bunch of little lemmings; if one person jumps off the end of a bridge you know they'll all follow.*

Maria was working hard at becoming something that her family and friends admired: a successful corporate employee. And when she wasn't happy with one great job she moved to the next great job. But she was playing roles other people wanted her to play.

Maria's career path led her through the lows of the 1990s recession and the highs of the dot-com bubble. Along the way, she managed to earn an MBA at the University of Southern California at Berkeley and get married. In 2000, Maria figured things were going pretty well.

■ Starting from Scratch

"You never know how long the rest of your life will be," Maria says, her voice full of the passion when talking about her friend who, on his way to a sales meeting, died in the jet that crashed into the Pentagon on September 11. His death shook her deeply. A few months later she was laid off from a failed dot-com. Maria knew she could have just looked for another job, but she didn't want to spend the rest of her life working for someone else in a job that someone else could just take away from her. She started asking herself, "What do I want to spend the rest of my life doing?"

Searching for a fulfilling career move, Maria turned within. Finally, she wasn't looking to what other people thought she should do. After her dot-com job went bust, she decided to "take the rest of the month off." Like me, a fan of self-help books, Maria turned to those books now. She also sought career counseling. She even took a "shamanic journey" in a college gymnasium, where a spiritual guide led her and others in deep meditation in order to get in touch with their deep instincts. For Native Americans, shamanic journeys once helped a tribe's leaders divine where to hunt for food and make other crucial decisions for the future of the tribe. Maria began her journey searching for a career that she would truly love, doing what she loved by looking to *harness what she had.*

"I tried to find out what I gravitate toward, what I like," she recalls. As ludicrous as it may have sounded, she decided what she really liked was shopping and traveling, neither of which she could do much of while unemployed. It seemed she was doomed to work for others in order to earn the money to do what she enjoyed. But why couldn't she do what she enjoyed *and* earn money?

The answer came suddenly: "I woke up one day and it was right in front of my face: This is what I'm going to do—start a shoe boutique."

Back when Maria was struggling to find what she loved to do, she had read a book that advised asking family members what they thought she was good at. Her sister's answer was ironic: "Maria likes achievement." Now, Maria was set to achieve something big. But this time, it "felt great"—she was taking a calculated risk and achieving something for herself, not for another company.

■ Underestimating Obstacles

Without spending a dime on market research, Maria knew an important thing about the Los Angeles shoe world: No one sold the kinds of handmade Italian shoes that she was used to buying in San Francisco nearly 300 miles away. These were the kinds of shoes that were a step above cookie-cutter department store brands but more affordable than high-end $500 Manolo Blahniks. (Incidentally, when my wife heard this story she told me the same thing about where we live in Atlanta.) Maria took advantage of common market knowledge that was not being put into business practice, a common thread among successful entrepreneurs.

Once she found what she loved, Maria worked fast. First, she subscribed to a weekly trade publication, *Footwear News.* Second, she went to the publication's Web site and found a shoe and accessory trade show in Paris. Third, she hopped on a jet to Paris.

On her trip to Paris, banking on her final commission check that she hoped would come in, Maria ordered tens of thousands of dollars worth of handmade Italian shoes and handbags.

"I didn't even have retail space. I just gave people my home address for shipments, thinking I'd just put it in my garage until I figured out where I was going to open up a store," she recalls. Then came the rude awakening of trying to find retail space in Los Angeles. "But I wasn't worried; I just knew it was something I had to take care of."

Finding a location in high-rent LA was a big obstacle. But once Maria was swept up in the love she had for shoes, the location problem seemed to shrink to manageable size. "I figured I was just going to start taking action and moving forward and I'd find a location," she recalls. "And that's pretty much what happened."

The problem was that most of the storefronts in great locations were out of her budget. And the ones within her budget weren't swarming with shoppers. So she took a bold move and rented a storefront on a block of Ventura Boulevard that had only one other store on it. "When I found it, it wasn't a destination location," Maria recalls. It felt like a good gamble.

Maria was excited and full of plans. Starting her own boutique reminded her of the joy she felt as a kid when she sold beaded necklaces door-to-door, or of her teen years when she ran a neighborhood babysitting service. Back then, she didn't even need the money and gave much of it away to charity. Now, as an adult, she could take her love of shoes, of travel, and of running a business and pour it all into her own company.

Even though she had an MBA, she enrolled in a community education course and used the syllabus to write her business plan. One by one, Maria checked off the items on her to-do list. She worked 16-hour days, doing absolutely everything herself.

"One of my girlfriends thought I was crazy," Maria says. "She actually told me, 'You don't want to start a shoe store.'" Listening to her inner hunter, Maria absolutely knew that she *did* want to start a shoe store. "I realized I can't listen to what other people tell me or I'll never be happy; I'd always be living my life for somebody else."

■ Building Momentum

Even though she was determined to listen to her instincts, Maria knew eventually she had to get help from other people. She referred again to the pages of *Footwear News,* an industry-specific trade magazine that proved an invaluable resource for finding vendors, publicists, freight forwarders, and people looking for shoe industry jobs.

Maria named her business Debout (pronounced duh-boo), a French word that means "to stand up," because her handmade shoes are easy to stand up in and look good in—plus the foreign name lets people know they're not going to see the kinds of shoes they see at the mall. After all, Maria wanted the kind of customer who wanted something different. While most people are afraid of unusual things—which is why chain restaurants like McDonald's are so popular—there are plenty of folks who want something exotic.

Early on, Maria learned how to get the word out to customers— thanks to a direct mail effort that flopped. She bought a mailing list of 10,000 names of people living in her store's immediate area and sent out flyers. The return rate was dismal: less than 1 percent. After that, Maria started keeping a database of customers; anyone who had ever bought from her went on that list. When she mails to that group, she has a whopping 10 percent return and more.

It turns out Maria wasn't the only Angelino hungry for unique shoes. In its first year, Debout shoes was profitable. In its second year, it more than doubled the first year's revenue. By the third year, it tripled the first year's revenue, and Maria was earning the six-figure income of her dot-com days. Why was she profitable so fast?

"I think a lot of it is the buying," Maria says. "I really go out of my way to go to places in Italy that nobody would even think of going unless they had contacts in this business."

Maria's unique line of shoes also gets a lot of attention from fashion magazines. Some of the big names, like *In Style, Lucky, People,* and *Us Weekly,* have run pieces on Maria's store.

LA's television industry also brings in a good chunk of Maria's clientele. When stylists for some of TV's biggest shows want unusual shoes for their characters' wardrobes, they shop at Debout. "You know that handbag Phoebe was carrying on the final episode of *Friends?* That came from my store," Maria says proudly.

Maria's love of the business even seems to help her store's block, which had only one other store on it when she signed her lease. "I decided to jump in and then other stores just joined in. After I came in there were two nice stores, then three, four, and now there are six."

It just goes to show that people who love what they do are a magnet for success.

■ Taking the Next Leap

In the beginning, Maria didn't hire any employees. Instead, she ran the shop and got help from a bunch of independent contractors: a photographer, a Web site developer, a graphic designer, and a press agent. Those folks have been with her since the early days. Now in her fourth year, Maria has worked up to six full-time employees: a manager, four salespeople, and a bookkeeper.

Maria still does the buying herself, going off on "shoe adventures" several times a year. On these adventures through Paris, northern Italy, and Milan, she sometimes combines business with pleasure and brings along her husband to do some sightseeing. With a life like this, Maria says she's actually glad she went through such a difficult time before starting Debout.

"If I had stayed in San Francisco in my cushy secure job, making a cushy secure low six figures, I probably never would have done this. I probably would have stayed working for somebody else," Maria says. "It kind of took the rug being pulled out from under me, losing my job, for me to wake up and say, 'Oh my God! I don't want another job that someone can take away from me. I want to do something I enjoy and make money at it.'"

Nowadays, all Maria's efforts go into building a business that's worth something. Everything goes into her brand. Her plan is to do something new every year. Last year it was selling product off of her Web site; next year she plans a second location. But she's taking it slow, because, she says, "the whole idea for leaving a corporate job was to have less stress." When it's time to launch something new, she trusts her instincts to tell her what's right.

And in the end, if you can find what you love, the rest of the pieces will fall into place.

■ Chapter Two

Dany Levy, Founder of *DailyCandy*

Desperately Seeking Challenge

I was lucky to get an e-mail from her at 3:30 AM to schedule our meeting for the next day. Catching up with Dany Levy is like trapping lightning in a bottle. And it's no wonder. At the age of 33, Levy—editor-in-chief and founder of *DailyCandy*—is responsible for nine brand-new e-mail publications every day of the week. With that kind of schedule, I'd be up at 3:30 every morning, too!

Stifled by her career writing for fashion magazines, Dany Levy launched her own online magazine and hasn't looked back. She has taken the New York publishing world by storm and has become a daily fixture for nearly a million subscribers around the world. What you will learn from this story is that if you are willing to grow and LEARN, at all costs, phenomenal things can happen.

All her life, Dany loved challenges and learning. New York's magazine world seemed like a challenge at first, but after four years she was bored and frustrated. Part of the problem was the three-month lead time of most magazines. Her start-up, an e-zine named *DailyCandy,* gave her the challenge she so desperately sought.

It's not that she didn't love working for lifestyle magazines—at first. After college, New York's fashion and style beat seemed exciting to Dany. After graduating from Brown University, she landed a three-month unpaid internship at *New York* magazine. She did the unglamorous gofer jobs like making coffee runs for editors and working the copy machine. But she also pitched ideas for articles and was actually able to write a few features. It was a time of great learning. She would see how her articles had been edited and changed and learn how to do better next time. Dany also learned from the article ideas that editors shot down: they were topics that had already been done before or were too broad. "It was an incredible experience," she recalls.

Four months later, Dany ended up working at *New York* magazine as the managing editor's assistant. She watched the managing editor deal with everyday details, such as how many pages would be in the next issue of the magazine, what to do when contract editors called with a problem getting their check, what to do when a new ad came in at the last minute and added pages that needed to be filled with content. Most important, she saw how the editor decided on each edition's lineup of articles, which was much like acting as the producer for a movie.

At first, Dany was happy just to learn without sticking her neck out. Then one day it all changed. It happened when she was doing her usual job of answering the phone. There was a rambling voice mail from a woman cursing the magazine and claiming she was Courtney Love. Calls from people claiming to be celebrities are pretty common, but Dany had a hunch this one was for real. Even though she could have been wrong and wasting the editor's time, she went to his office and played the voice mail for him.

It turned out that Dany was right: it really was Courtney Love. The editor had her transcribe the voice-mail message, and the magazine ran the text as a magazine piece. It happened that Love had mistaken them for their competitor, *The New Yorker,* which had done a scathing piece about her. It was just the kind of gossipy tidbit that readers love. Dany ended up doing a television interview talking about the experience with *Extra!* She did well enough that the magazine started having her appear on morning news shows to discuss their latest stories. She quickly learned not to fidget on camera, and about the power of selling magazines on air.

Like a lot of people in their late 20s, Dany's learning curve started to flatten out after the first few years in her career. She had more opportunities, but she never regained the excitement of those early days. The worst came when she took a job as beauty editor for *Self* magazine, where she ended up mostly schmoozing with advertisers and writing very little. Even her next gig freelancing for magazines and the *New York Times* was stifling: Dany was a people person, and she felt trapped writing alone all day in her apartment. Both polar extremes in job duties left her unfulfilled.

The idea for *DailyCandy* came to her in the fall of 1999, when she was working on the prototype of *Lucky*, a Condé Nast magazine. It was a job that many people would have killed for, but Dany still felt bored writing fashion captions, something she could do in her sleep by that point in her career. For a moment Dany considered going back to school for her MBA but then decided that instead of studying about business from books, she would learn business by going to work and creating a company of her own. A million readers later, turns out starting *DailyCandy* was the right move!

The day before Christmas of 1999, Dany made the leap and quit Condé Nast to start her own venture using money she'd saved for business school. Now her real education would begin.

■ Starting from Scratch

"I've always been a 'shoulda been done yesterday' kind of person," Dany says. Her friends tell her she doesn't mull things over very long and doesn't hem and haw, which is why they like shopping with her. When it came to *DailyCandy*, she was no different. "I couldn't *not* pursue this idea that I'd got in my head," Dany says. "I couldn't fight it." Some people are motivated by fear of failure; people like Dany are motivated by the fear of not achieving something big.

The idea in Dany's head was a brief daily e-mail that women could look forward to opening each morning—like a little piece of candy, *DailyCandy.* Because it was e-mail, not print, she would avoid the long production schedule and high printing costs of magazines. And a daily e-mail was something she could do by herself, without a huge staff.

On January 3, 2000, Dany sat down at her desk and typed a two-page description of her e-zine. On May 6, she launched.

Those three months working on *DailyCandy*'s launch were a blur of activity. First thing was to come up with the right tone. For that, Dany harnessed what she had: her college experiences writing poetry and fiction for her creative writing program at Brown University. For a few semesters she had turned inward, going through her "dark, writerly phase," as she calls it. After classes, she would come home to her apartment, cook dinner, and write for hours. Mainly she wrote stream-of-consciousness fiction, where she tried to write from the point of view of different voices—serious stuff—and she didn't really use that skill in her magazine work.

For *DailyCandy,* Dany harnessed that skill and created a sort of fictional character that she thinks of as "the *DailyCandy* girl." In her mind, the *DailyCandy* girl is a breezy, smart young woman clueing in her friends about her fashion find of the day, like the woman who calls up her best friend and tells her, "Guess what, I found a great new spa that just opened." Each day, *DailyCandy* would play the game of show-and-tell, sharing a new fashion or lifestyle tip learned just that day.

Next she had to build a subscriber list. To do that, Dany found a friend who could set up a Web page and draw a sample page of what the e-mail would look like: a cyber version of a pen-and-ink drawing tinted with bright watercolors and picturing a young woman walking a little dog on a city street. Dany sent the sample page to everyone she knew, asking them to forward it to everyone they could think of.

In March, the first issue launched with a drawing of that same young woman walking down a city street with a baguette in one hand and a bag of fresh groceries dangling from the other. The article was a bit about the highlights from a new guide to New York City's nightlife. That first day, *DailyCandy* started out with 700 subscribers.

For almost an entire year, Dany wrote nearly the whole thing, with a little help from friends and two other writers. She wasn't making any money, just building the brand. She still needed to figure out where the money would come from.

■ Underestimating Obstacles

Following the magazine world's business model, Dany figured she would get money from advertisers. But for sponsors to take her seriously, *DailyCandy* needed a lot of subscribers. So Dany resolved to grow subscribers in the lowest-cost way she could: putting a "send to a friend" button at the bottom of each *DailyCandy* page. "That forward button is so incredibly powerful," Dany says. Also at the bottom of each page was a "sign up for *DailyCandy*" button, shaped like a piece of candy. Thanks to her first 700 subscribers forwarding the e-mail to friends, *DailyCandy* was getting between 100 and 200 new subscribers each day.

Those were busy days for Dany. *DailyCandy* wasn't her only project; she was still freelancing in order to earn money to live on. Her days were filled with two jobs: writing articles for pay and staying on top of trends so she would have a *DailyCandy* e-mail to send out each day. Dany found some help through friends. One friend did some of the research and fact-checking for an hourly fee. Another friend helped her write up financial projections. Instead of being exhausted, Dany was exhilarated. To this day, Dany finds herself waking up in the middle of the night with ideas that she just has to do. So she goes with it. If she's up at 3 AM with an idea, she just makes herself a cup of tea and jots it down.

One of those middle-of-the-night ideas was to launch in other cities—that was a sure way to add subscribers. The first edition she added was Los Angeles, because it seemed to have a big population of young, fashion-conscious women looking for the next new thing. Dany spent some time in LA interviewing writers and deciding on an editor and then teaching her the *DailyCandy* tone.

One day, she realized she was on the right track with growing subscriptions. It happened in mid-May 2000, just two months after she'd launched. Dany did something unusual and recommended a book, *Sam the Cat and Other Stories.* It was an edgy book of stories about New York's dating scene from the point of view of young, neurotic men. The day of the *DailyCandy* feature, the book sold out in two Manhattan bookstores by noon. The book also shot up to number 38 on the Amazon.com bestseller list that day, up from 10,000 the previous evening.

Dany didn't take any money for recommending products or stores in her daily e-mail, but vendors were now clamoring to be included on her site. She was starting to be a media force.

■ Building Momentum

Even though she was running *DailyCandy* out of her New York apartment, Dany knew she couldn't do it that way for long. She needed a team of full-time employees, especially people with business know-how. Luckily, Dany found e-commerce whiz Pete Sheinbaum, who said he would handle the business side of things for three months while working remotely from Boulder, Colorado. Sheinbaum had a great résumé; he'd been E! Online's commerce manager and had come up with a new e-business model for that cable television station. Dany figured he could find a way to turn *DailyCandy* into a real business.

But early on, Pete taught Dany something about business that had nothing to do with number crunching. It had to do with how an entrepreneur deals with his network. One day, when Pete sent her some business projections, Dany excitedly asked him to teach her how to crunch numbers. His answer: "No, that's not what you're here for." Gently, Pete reminded Dany that no entrepreneur can be responsible for the whole project. When you partner with someone to do a job, you need to trust that person to do it—not try to take over everything.

It was an important lesson that came in handy when Dany was hiring editors. At first, she wrote everything for *DailyCandy*'s New York edition herself. Coming up with ideas and articles was no problem for Dany, who had been working in the New York fashion world since she was 21. But her business plan was about growing. For a while it was just herself and two other women writers working in New York, with Pete on the speakerphone from Boulder. The three women used to joke that they were like *Charlie's Angels*, the television series where the boss, Charlie, always gave the female trio instructions for their latest crime-solving assignment via telephone. Dany was having fun.

And *DailyCandy* was earning money. The first advertiser was Redken, an upscale beauty supply brand. *DailyCandy*'s e-mail ads were sent out each day separately from the daily e-mail.

A year and a half after she'd launched it, *DailyCandy* was profitable. Pete had agreed to stay for a year and a half and had hit on a business model that was 100 percent based on ad revenues. Subscribers get the magazine for free, while advertisers pay for advertising. Dany didn't realize it at first, but she'd managed to attract a demographic that was incredibly attractive to advertisers: educated, high-income women who are between ages 24 and 35 and love to shop.

On September 11, 2001, when terrorists attacked New York's twin towers, *DailyCandy* became a sort of valentine to Manhattan. That day's e-mail was simply a heartfelt message of condolence to the victims and their families. The next day *DailyCandy* told readers where to get "I love New York" T-shirts and merchandise. Dany even made some television appearances as a sort of poster girl for the city. For the rest of September, when there weren't many new store openings or galas to write about, her e-mails included ideas for how to help lower Manhattan merchants, such as ordering a case of wine from a Manhattan liquor store.

Soon after, Dany started adding on more editions. To grow her network of writers, Dany reached out to her network of college and work friends. Gradually, *DailyCandy* grew to include 11 editions—including a weekly kid's edition with ideas for gifts and products for children and a travel edition—and is now sending its daily e-mails to nearly a million subscribers.

When it comes to hiring, Dany's experience brings up a good point: If you take the time to find and hire good people, you should be able to trust them to do their job. At first, she admits she was guilty of looking over her editors' shoulders, but she learned to let go. After all, *DailyCandy* isn't about what Dany likes but about the tastes of the fictional *DailyCandy* girl. So, Dany reminds herself to trust her editors and let them decide what's important in their city's edition. For example, Dany wouldn't go out and buy dangly earrings or a Fendi handbag, but *DailyCandy*'s readers would. So Dany seeks out editors who have definite tastes and remembers to empower them to have good judgment.

■ Taking the Next Leap

As the brand grows, Dany finds herself having to make decisions about how involved she is going to be and how much she is going to delegate. In the beginning, she was doing all the media appearances and interviews. After all, she knew how to do this, thanks to her days at *New York* magazine when she appeared on morning news shows to talk about the latest magazine edition. But just because an entrepreneur can do a job doesn't mean he or she should. Dany realized it was in her best interest to make sure that *DailyCandy* wasn't identified with one "face."

In start-ups, how a business is viewed by the customer is a big thing to consider. You may want to live your brand, or you may want to be more behind the scenes, like Dany. After all, if a founder hopes to one day sell the company, it may not be worth as much to a buyer if the founder's name and face are too tied up in the brand. And if something happens to the founder, it can hurt the company.

So Dany started letting other people make the public appearances and interviews. She doesn't want to be synonymous with *DailyCandy*. And she wants to launch editions in more and more cities.

As *DailyCandy* grows, Dany continues to harness what she has and learn more—she uses her writing and editing expertise to oversee the writers, and she uses her network from her days at Condé Nast and *New York* magazine.

A year and a half ago, Dany made a big decision about growing *DailyCandy*. She sold part of her company to the Pilot Group, a private equity fund headed by Bob Pittman who started MTV in the 1980s and reinvigorated the Six Flags theme parks. Part of that deal was to get her friend and first chief operating officer, Pete Sheinbaum, to leave Boulder and come to New York. Now *DailyCandy* is poised to "own" its online niche. In 2005, it launched a London edition, *DailyCandy London*.

Recently, Dany found the two-page description of her vision for *DailyCandy* that she had written five years ago. She wanted it to be a quick, fun read with nice-looking graphics, something that busy women would forward on to friends. Since it was Internet-based, she wanted to come up with new stories before the newspapers and magazines found out about them. The tone would be fun and intelligent, delivering a light-hearted tidbit to subscriber's mailboxes each day. It turns out it's very close to what *DailyCandy* is today and shows the strength of her vision.

Besides overseeing *DailyCandy* (Dany jokes that her title is "quality inspector number 462"), she still does a little freelance writing and tries to spend time mentoring many of the young college graduates who send her e-mails asking for advice in their writing careers. "That's how I got where I am," Dany says. "People took the time to talk to me."

When it comes to the future, Dany isn't sure what she'll do. Even though she sounds like a fiercely driven entrepreneur, she wouldn't mind settling down one day and starting a family—guys, good luck slowing her down. Her next challenge is trying to figure out the delicate balance between work and life, and juggling nine new publications a day and running a business should keep her learning curve as steep as it has ever been.

■ Chapter Three

Dave Helfrich, Founder of **Colorworks Development**

Confidence

I'm excited to tell the story about Dave Helfrich because, unlike my other subjects, I worked for him. Or, stated more clearly, I learned to work for myself because of Dave. Heading into my sophomore summer at UNC-Chapel Hill, I decided to forgo the coveted investment banking internship at Merrill Lynch and become a painter—that's painter as in house painter, not as in artist.

Dave's entrepreneurial story begins at Michigan State, somewhere between the rinse and spin cycles at the Splish Splash Laundromat. Dave figured he just had to find a way to get out of washing his own clothes. Freshman year at Michigan State was the first time he'd had to do laundry. And it was a drag. "I could cook, I could clean, but I hated doing laundry," he recalls. His parents told him he'd just have to buckle down and wash his clothes, but then Dave hated people telling him what to do almost as much as he hated washing his clothes.

What's a teenager to do? Pay someone else to do it? The problem was, everyone he knew hated doing laundry—and the Splish Splash wash-and-fold service wasn't included in the weekly allowance from his parents. That's when Dave's entrepreneurial mind-set kicked in.

Dave loved making money. In high school he spent summers on his paper route, washing cars, and staining decks. "I was always looking for ways to make money," says Dave, and he laughs when he says it because, well, his love of money got him over his hatred of washing clothes. Early on, Dave was learning what I call the art of the HUNT.

■ Starting from Scratch

Picture an 18-year-old Dave happily walking through the dormitories on Mondays after classes, gathering up bagfuls of laundry and stuffing them into his car. On Thursday he would drive back to the laundry service to pick up the clothes—washed and folded—and deliver them to his student customers. For this service, dubbed The Clothes Line, Dave charged $300 per semester. He had a business partner and hired helpers, and eventually even had a driver and a business manager. At the end of that first year, Dave's laundry delivery service earned $15,000.

This story sounds so rosy that it may be a surprise to learn that only a few years after graduating (and selling his laundry business for $50,000!), Dave made some career decisions that got people second-guessing his judgment. But Dave persevered because his college laundry service gave him something far more crucial to survival as an entrepreneur than its selling price, something in short supply in this world: confidence and self-assurance. Dave was going to need both.

For entrepreneurs like Dave, the first part of the Hunt for success is harnessing what you have. That isn't to say that you should ignore your shortcomings. Certainly you should be aware of them and seek improvement. But in mastering the art of the HUNT, you've got to build on your strengths—and Dave's strength was that he was a natural dealmaker. He also had the self-confidence to rely on his dealmaking strength.

Dave's dealmaking ability includes a knack for zeroing in on what people want and how much they're willing to pay. Whether it's clean clothes delivered to their dorm rooms or a contract to supply computer parts to an industry giant—a deal's a deal—and Dave likes doing deals. And he likes using that talent.

Now he needed to learn to make a living from that skill.

■ Underestimating Obstacles

At first, life after graduation seemed like a series of quick successes for Dave. He landed a college internship at IBM, although he had to postpone graduation by a few months in order to take advantage of it. After graduation, he got a job as buyer for the computer giant. His first assignment was to travel to Taiwan, Singapore, and Malaysia to get the best deal possible to build a computer mouse. There he was, 22 years old, boarding an airplane for Taiwan to negotiate a multi-million-dollar contract. He traveled alone because IBM's budget for the mouse wasn't big enough to accommodate two employees. Dave didn't know the language and wasn't sure how he was going to find his hotel room or his office. "It was kind of scary," Dave admits.

When it came time to negotiate, Dave pulled out all the stops and did everything he knew to get the price down. The good news: Dave saved IBM $5 million in his first deal. Better news: Dave leapfrogged several rungs of the corporate ladder and became international commodity manager for IBM's AC adapter and batteries for the ThinkPad brand.

In the culture at IBM, folks have a way of describing high-performing guys like Dave: they walk on water. Dave was two years into his tenure at IBM, the youngest person on the procurement team, and walking on water. That's when the bad news hit.

"I worked with great people at IBM and learned a lot," Dave says. "But at the end of the day, I was getting the traditional raises based on the scales in corporate America. I reminded my manager that I'd saved the company $55 million. He said, 'David, I can't give you any more money. You've maxed out.'"

Now, a $50,000 salary and the opportunity to travel around the world doesn't seem too bad for a 24-year-old. But the situation rankled Dave. It made him remember his father's slaving away in corporate America, coming home each night complaining about his boss and the decisions made by people over his head. "I didn't want to go through what my father went through," Dave says. "What controlled his life was his boss."

Dave tried to get around this corporate obstacle by making a deal with his manager: "I told him not to pay me a salary but to pay me a percentage of what I saved the company. Maybe it was a little boastful, but I wanted to be paid on my performance. I've negotiated across the table with people from Toshiba or Sanyo, and these salespeople have made hundreds of thousands of dollars in commissions off what they've negotiated with me. But when I negotiated with my manager, all I got was my $50,000 salary."

Even though his argument was excellent, Dave didn't get the raise he wanted. Not even close. The obstacles to wealth at IBM were too great for Dave, but he didn't give up. Although he didn't quit right away, he started calling around and looking for another job. What he came up with was yet another corporate job and an interview at Whirlpool, but he had a feeling that wouldn't make him happy either. He knew that somehow he would find a way around this obstacle to wealth.

▪ Building Momentum

Back in Michigan and fresh from Whirlpool's headquarters, Dave stopped to visit with an old college buddy who ran a house-painting franchise. It was second nature to Dave to visit with his old friend. He knew how important it was to maintain a network of friends and contacts. Now, when he was at a low point, Dave leaned on his friend and told him about his unhappiness at IBM.

Listening to his friend talk about his painting business, Dave saw a solution. Right there at lunch, he took some bold steps. "I came to the realization that a corporate job wouldn't work out. I looked at the opportunities painting single-family houses, and I thought this might be it." Dave didn't plan on spending much time on ladders; he figured painting homes was a scalable business and he could sell franchises to other people. So he plotted his break with corporate America and bought a master franchise from Colorworks for three states, selling franchise rights and collecting royalties. It seemed like a good move.

Not everyone thought so.

"My parents thought I was crazy," Dave recalls, an edge coming into his voice when he remembers how ridiculous it sounded back then. After all, he had a glamorous job jetting around the world for IBM, and he was leaving that stability and prestige to start a franchise business painting houses. "I'm going to start a painting company," he would say, his voice blunt, humorless, and braced for the criticism he knew people would have. "I'm going to hire college kids and we're going to paint houses."

At first, Dave's network wasn't supportive of his painting plan. So he built himself up with the confidence he'd gained in his earlier laundry business and with some of his business contacts—especially the other disenchanted IBMers who were starting off on their own. And he also looked back on his success with his college laundry business, which had helped him build financial security. Instead of graduating from college with debt and loans, he graduated with a secure nest egg.

He also had some knowledge of the house-painting business. The summer after his junior year, just like me at Carolina, Dave painted close to 70 houses with 15 employees and took home $24,000 working for Triple A Student Painters. Working as a supervisor, he learned that "business isn't always fun, and business isn't always easy. There's hiring and firing people and meeting the customer's expectations."

In the painting franchise, he could draw on his network of contacts from the college job, but he was still a little doubtful. What if the painting business was just a nostalgic step backward to his college days? Like most of us, Dave could fall into an unthinking habit of defining himself by what he did. When we introduce ourselves at parties we say our names and add, "I'm a lawyer," "I'm a doctor," or "I'm head of procurement at IBM." Somehow, "I run a house-painting business" doesn't have the same ring to it.

Still, Dave held on to his confidence and set to work, keeping in touch with his enthusiastic friend at Colorworks.

■ Taking the Next Leap

Even now, knowing that the story ended happily, Dave looks tired when he thinks about his first steps in the painting business. Buying the franchise was one thing; making it work was another. "Nothing ever came easy," he says. For the first few months, he held onto his IBM job. For Dave, having a reliable income was vital. It felt too risky to depend on the painting business for his livelihood.

It was a good first step for Dave, but it meant long days. First, he would put in a full day at the office, then drive two or three hours round-trip to college campuses to recruit students for the painting business. Finally, when money was coming in from the painting business, he quit IBM.

"Those first two years were the toughest," Dave says. "I do remember wondering if I was ever going to make it. For me the fear of failing was my biggest motivator. I didn't want to fail." In private, he had many a sleepless night at the thought of losing his shirt. "I'd left IBM, I'd left a great job, and I had a house payment and a car payment. Early on it was a struggle."

During those tough times, he drew on the memory of his college successes. In his sophomore year, Dave noticed everyone wanted cool sunglasses. The kind that went for $100 or more at the mall. Dave wondered if there was a way he could undercut those prices for college students like himself who wanted nice things but depended on checks from Mom and Dad. Parents, after all, aren't too keen on finding out their kids spent $100 for a pair of sunglasses. So he came up with a simple plan: sell sunglasses on campus—with barely any overhead—for half what they cost at the mall.

Along with another student, he called around and set up a distributorship—with Ray-Ban and Vuarnet—on the campuses of Michigan State and the University of Michigan. He bought the sunglasses wholesale, then marked them up 100 percent and held a one-day sale in the Student Union. In the end, he had a nice collection of sunglasses and a $10,000 profit *in just one day.*

During his tough early days with Colorworks, Dave persevered by recalling his early successes in simple businesses like laundering and sales. He also focused on making good deals and outsourcing much of the work. In the first year, Dave's Colorworks business brought in $300,000 in sales. After expenses, he was left with about the same amount of money he would have had from his salary at IBM—about $50,000. It wasn't a fortune, but at least the business was profitable. The second year, sales were up to $500,000, and he was able to hire some regional managers. By the fourth year, he was breathing easy and breaking $1 million in revenue. Most important, Dave was growing his net worth.

While his painting business was successful enough for any entrepreneur, Dave continued to expand his business and ventured into apartment renovation. Using the same business model he'd had in the painting business, he outsourced much of the renovating work to subcontractors and hired only about five full-time employees, later taking on a business partner. It was a business model that clearly worked. After two years, he found opportunities for larger projects and new apartment construction.

Meanwhile, the painting business reached a point where it was bringing in $2.5 million in sales, with regional managers running it. Having built the business as far as he thought it could go, he started looking for bigger opportunities in construction and development. He sold his painting franchise portion of Colorworks and invested the profits into his new construction venture, Colorworks Development.

Now, Dave's construction company Colorworks Development is worth about $10 million. He and a joint venture partner have $100 million of development deals in the pipeline, and he keeps looking for more. Looking back, he says that earning that first million was the hardest.

For Dave, learning confidence in his abilities early on enabled him to leap from the corporate world to entrepreneurship. He chose to harness what he had—exceptional dealmaking ability—and not focus on his unhappiness with the restrictions inherent in a large organization. This is actually the opposite of what we're often told. If you've ever had a performance review on a job, I'll bet you've discussed weaknesses that were areas for improvement. In fact, most people, if asked to make a list of their own strengths and weaknesses, can identify more weaknesses than strengths.

Dave's story shows the power of confidence. Well-placed confidence can help overcome all sorts of obstacles. Dave's confidence allowed him to leave an unhappy situation—even if it was a glamorous job jetting around the world—to start a painting company, even if it meant starting over again on the bottom rung of the success ladder. "Sometimes," Dave says, "that's where you have to start."

Stepping away from the safety and prestige of a corporate job took a lot of confidence and self-assurance. Luckily, Dave had nurtured that confidence throughout his teens and early 20s with some steady successes. Each of those successes not only put cash in his pocket but also put confidence in his heart.

When I first met Dave, he was basically just as poor as me, living in college. Ten years later he's worth about $10 million—proof that the right amount of confidence can go a very long way.

■ Chapter Four

Ian Gerard, Cofounder of **Gen Art** ■

Common Vision

Staring at a black-and-white art print hanging on a friend's wall, Ian Gerard came up with an idea that would save him from a law career he already hated.

During the recession of the early 1990s, Ian was going to law school and commiserating with his old friends. As he watched them in their job struggles, Ian saw them fall into two groups: the haves and have-nots. For the art majors, it was bad. "The art market had completely cracked, galleries were not taking risks on new talent," Ian recalls. Then he had another group of friends working in Manhattan's financial district, earning enough disposable income to replace their dorm room posters with boring framed reproductions.

It wasn't that his suit-and-tie friends didn't want original artwork; "they just assumed if they walked through a gallery in New York everything would cost $10,000 or more," Ian says, so they settled for canned art. "They didn't realize that for just a little more they could go out and buy original artwork by somebody in their peer group. So I kind of put the two together."

Ian's plan: put on a big splashy art show for young artists to show off their wares to other 20-somethings. Not only would they find great original art at good prices, they would be helping other people of their generation. He would call the effort "Gen Art" and urge people to "Join the Revolution!"

Gen Art has what I call "common vision." It's an idea that is simple and everyday—young people helping each other—but also visionary because it hasn't been done before. Many ideas can have common vision. The key is to share your common vision with other people. Gradually, as more people hold the vision in common, everyday vision grows in strength. In the right circumstances, common vision spreads like wildfire.

There was one glaring problem for Gen Art: Ian didn't know much about the art world. Sure, he'd grown up in Manhattan with parents who took him to art shows and museums, but Ian recalls he "was always the first guy to go sit down on the bench at the art gallery."

■ Starting from Scratch

While Ian lacked art expertise, he was excellent when it came to championing a good cause. And he knew that the idea of young people helping one another was a cause he could believe in.

Back in his junior year at Vassar College, Ian had been spurred to take up a cause after reading a conservative screed in a campus newspaper. It made his blood boil. Even now, talking about that article, he bristles. It wasn't just that one article. All the campus newspapers leaned too far to the right for Ian's taste. It didn't seem right; here he was, at a college so liberal its only course requirement was a foreign language, yet all its newspapers voiced conservative views.

Ian's plans quickly snowballed. He started out one day walking around campus with a pocketful of thumbtacks—posting flyers on bulletin boards. Within weeks he'd found advertisers and journalism students. What started out as Ian's private cause ended up being Vassar College's second biggest publication, *Left of Center*.

Now, Ian had another cause: young people helping artists of their own generation. What he needed next was some help getting it off the ground. The first people Ian inspired were his family. His younger brother Stefan saw that the idea was so simple and "nobody out there was doing it," Ian says. He knew his idea had a kind of common vision that he could harness.

■ Underestimating Obstacles

But there were problems. First off, they had no money. So the next step was to find someone to loan them some cash. They first asked their parents, who were convinced enough to loan them $5,000.

The next problem was expertise: neither Ian nor his brother knew much about visual arts. While Ian was the first to sit down at the bench at a museum, Stefan wasn't far behind. Lack of art expertise could have been a huge stumbling block; in fact, most people might think it odd that they would even think of taking on such a venture without art backgrounds. Instead, not having art expertise would end up helping them make the leap into business prospects that Ian and Stefan hadn't even thought of. As it turned out, art expertise would have held them back.

"It's more about mission," Ian says, "and not specific industries. It's a bizarre business model, but it makes sense."

So the brothers talked to some more friends, searching for advice about the art world. It turned out that art expertise was close at hand. Ian knew someone with close family ties to major contemporary art collectors, and he also found a young woman who had recently graduated from a prestigious university with a master's degree in art history.

Instead of focusing on his weaknesses, Ian hit on his strengths: believing in a good cause and having a supportive family and a great social network. And suddenly, the first stumbling blocks didn't seem so big after all.

"I learned that I have to make a million decisions every day," says Ian. "I have to have the confidence that they are the right ones, even if they occasionally turn out not to be. You have to have that confidence to take action."

■ Building Momentum

In the beginning, Ian was a law student, Stefan had a publishing job, and their friends had various jobs, mostly in New York's finance industry. With their little bit of cash and art expertise, the group set up shop in Ian's dorm room kitchen. The snowball started to roll. When his roommates would get up for their morning coffee, "there'd be somebody they didn't know working on a laptop at the kitchen table," Ian recalls.

Like most successful entrepreneurs, Ian was keenly aware of his network and tended it like a well-kept garden. He knew that you can get anything you want in life if you just help enough other people get what they want.

Ian had grown up in New York City, a place crawling with successful artists. And he knew that some of those artists would want to take up his cause of helping the next generation. In fact, he had a hunch that there were artists who would be flattered to be asked. Gradually, the asking paid off. Gen Art built a 20-person advisory board of successful artists from the 1970s and 1980s, art dealers, and gallery owners. Now it wasn't just a good idea anymore, "it was a good idea that was endorsed by blue chip art world people," Ian says. "That was critical."

Once they had art advisors lined up, Ian felt they needed something more than artwork to get the attention of young people. As he puts it: "Art is not always sexy, so we wanted to sex it up a little bit."

Again, Ian looked around at his hometown of Manhattan, the kind of place where an afternoon stroll often leads right to the set of a DeNiro movie or a supermodel photo shoot. Ian and his friends thought nothing of bumping into movie stars and models at restaurants and nightclubs. They had plenty of them in their network. And what do models and movie stars enjoy? Good causes and a chance to show off their stuff.

So Ian and his friends started contacting everyone they could in their well-tended networks, looking for young, beautiful people who wanted to be associated with their cause. They ended up with Caroline Herreras Jr. and Tatiana Von Furstenberg agreeing to be honorary hosts of the Gen Art fundraiser. Not bad for a few weeks' worth of phone calls.

◼ Taking the Next Leap

Gen Art started out as a good idea with a quirky business plan and no clear source of cash. Gradually, as it grew with the support of an advisory board, Gen Art took its first step: a fundraiser.

Ian and his friends plastered Manhattan with flyers advertising the fundraiser. It reminded him of his college days, when he started a student newspaper by posting flyers on bulletin boards. He wasn't sure where he was going with Gen Art, but he knew he was enjoying the ride.

When the night of the fundraiser arrived, it was sold out. Five hundred young people crammed into a penthouse to see the work of four young artists—and, to be honest, a glimpse of the celebrity hosts. The fundraiser didn't just raise a lot of money, it earned Gen Art its first piece of press: a glowing review in the *New York Times* Style section.

"It was a big bonding experience," Ian recalls. Here was a group of young people supporting their peers, working for the common good, having a good time, and earning enough money to almost break even. Gen Art was halfway between a business and a hobby.

After that, they had to choose a location for their first art show. According to their advisors, SoHo was the center of the city's art world. So Gen Art's first event would be in an 8,000-square-foot storefront gallery on West Broadway, a very expensive location for such a fledgling venture.

"From day one, we would do as splashy an event as we could afford," recalls Ian. "We created an illusion of being more well funded than we were. I think that was important for people to take us seriously."

After that great beginning, things moved slowly and carefully, with the group of friends sharing a vision and working pro bono. "We would plan one thing and it would go well, then we would plan the next thing," Ian says. "For a year or two it was just 'Let's see how it goes'; we still weren't really a business." While there wasn't much income to support a staff, Ian's brother Stefan left his publishing job and started working full-time as Gen Art's "operations guy."

Meanwhile, Ian had graduated from law school, and "for the next three years I was a lawyer and helping run Gen Art at the same time," Ian recalls. While the other young lawyers at his firm put in grueling 16-hour days, Ian would do the minimum 9-to-5 day so he could work on Gen Art. "My secretary would always look at me kind of weird because I was getting calls from *Women's Wear Daily* and other publications at the office. There were more of those calls than there were calls from my clients."

Gen Art was Ian's passion. Even a bad day with Gen Art was better than a good day at the law office, especially when what looked like a huge screwup turned out to be a gold mine. The screwup began when a young fashion designer approached Ian and told him that young fashion designers faced enormous odds getting their work noticed—runway shows cost hundreds of thousands of dollars. Even though Ian dismissed the idea because he knew nothing about the fashion world, "the idea stuck in my head."

Months later, Gen Art was doing an art exhibition and Ian thought, *Hey, we have this big space, why don't we do a little fashion show?* Since they didn't have any fashion experience, the group didn't know such a thing was unheard of in the middle of the summer. If they had had some fashion expertise, they would have known that the sun rises and sets in the fashion world on one incredible week known as Fashion Week, an industry event held every February and September in New York. But the Gen Art folks didn't know about Fashion Week, so they blundered ahead with their fashion show featuring the work of some young designers. For Ian, it seemed like a logical leap. "Gen Art is about a generation supporting its peer group," he says. Young people can buy clothes from young designers just as they can buy art from young artists.

Logistically, it was a nightmare. The air-conditioning blew out, and hundreds of people couldn't get in. "At the end of it, I thought I was going to have a heart attack," Ian recalls. Three days later, when he was vowing never to do a fashion show again, *Women's Wear Daily* ran an article about the show, explaining why something like Gen Art was so needed in fashion. "That really made us forget about the pain and hardship and all the things we'd kind of screwed up," Ian says, "and realize that there was an opening here for somebody like us."

After the glowing article in *Women's Wear Daily*, Gen Art consulted with some fashion experts and started doing fashion shows "that weren't a nightmare," Ian says. At the same time, Gen Art franchised its business model to open locations in Los Angeles and San Francisco and added film festivals to its offerings. The Gen Art name was growing.

In late 1997, Ian left his law career (and six-figure salary) to jump headlong into running the then three-year-old Gen Art full-time. At that point, Gen Art was showing signs of evolving; instead of being supported by ticket sales, the company had a new income stream. The new business model was a cross between an event management company and an advertising agency, with corporate sponsors willing to commit large portions of their advertising budgets to sponsor fashion and art shows.

His first day on the job, Ian opened up the books and had a big shock: Gen Art was swimming in debt. Working at Gen Art part-time, he hadn't looked closely at the finances. Suddenly, he saw the whole picture: "Oh my God! I just left being a lawyer, I left my profession, and I came here and the books look like a mess. There's $35,000 on 13 different credit cards at 23 percent."

Ian took a deep breath and drew on what he'd learned in the first three years of taking Gen Art from a dream to a company. He worked at restructuring the debt and hunting for some bigger corporate sponsorships.

At the same time, Gen Art's fashion shows were attracting notice. Some of the designers they had shown, like Chaiken and Rebecca Taylor, were starting to pop. Ironically, the fashion shows— which started out as an afterthought—were winning Gen Art the most notice. And bigger corporate sponsors were listening to Gen Art's proposals. When Ralph Lauren and Finlandia Vodka jumped on board, Ian knew he was right to leave behind his law career.

Even with all the success, Ian found he had a chicken-and-egg kind of problem: Gen Art was too small for some of the big sponsors but needed these sponsors in order to grow bigger. By now, Ian was used to the steps of his hunt and knew that he could underestimate this obstacle. So he bluffed.

When Heineken said it wouldn't put its money into the venture unless it was in five markets, Ian announced it was opening offices in Chicago and Miami. In the harsh economic climate of 2002, Gen Art was expanding into two new offices that it couldn't really afford. But it got the Heineken contract and many more after that.

These days, Gen Art is a prosperous not-for-profit organization, putting on at least 100 shows a year and bringing in approximately $4 million in revenue in 2004. Whether it's a weeklong film festival, a star-studded fashion show, a DJ competition, or an art exhibition, Gen Art holds to its mission of young people helping their own generation. The next project is to expand into cyberspace with a new interactive Web site and e-mail newsletter.

Looking back on it all, Ian says his secret is finding a common vision and taking steps to make it a reality. That philosophy is something he still stands by today: "Don't just complain or come up with ideas; just go do it. If you have a good idea and follow through, good things can happen."

Chapter Five

Connie Grunwaldt, Realtor

Decisive Progression

This story about the residential real estate industry really hits home with me. My mother, after decades of raising four children full-time and working part-time in accounting, found her stride as a real estate agent. Now she loves what she does for a living, having found something that fits her charming personality. She basically works for herself and has been making a nice six-figure income since her second year!

The real estate industry continues to be explosive. If you have a warm personality, have the ability to really listen to what people are looking for, and find yourself looking at the home section of your weekend newspaper, then you may be able to make a fortune selling real estate and love it along the way. Secrets from Chicago real estate superstar Connie Grunwaldt may be the catalyst you have been looking for all along.

Even if you don't know what you want to do, Connie Grunwaldt is proof that progressing (positive inertia) is better than not moving at all. After 13 years slogging through corporate America—selling packaged goods—Connie jumped into a cushy career selling high-end residential real estate in Chicago.

In college, Connie was a typical type A overachiever—the kind of student that corporations love to recruit from campuses each spring. She thrived on the personality tests and the high-stakes interviews for promotions that greeted her in corporate America. In her early 20s, Connie found it thrilling. "I'm still a little bit of an adrenaline junkie," she says. "I kind of liked sitting on the edge of my seat with sweaty armpits so I couldn't take off my jacket during the interview."

In corporate America, that attitude gets you noticed. At Procter & Gamble, Connie rose from a plebe selling laundry detergent to management level in just two years. Later, at competitor S.C. Johnson, she kept climbing.

All this from someone who wasn't really sure what she wanted to be when she grew up. When Connie graduated from college with a degree in political science and international relations, she figured she'd work for a year and make some money before going to graduate school for something challenging. For her, a job would be a kind of sabbatical after her whirlwind college years keeping up an A average and serving in student government.

But Connie doesn't do anything halfway. When it came to looking for a job, she threw herself into getting the best job she could: a corporate job because that's how everyone she knew defined a great job.

She landed at Procter & Gamble after an arduous hiring process in which she was weeded out from 600 other applicants. "I felt so thrilled and special," she says. Connie, who had tended bar in college and worked at a car wash in high school, didn't mind the unglamorous side of her job: meeting with grocers and getting pushed around in the rough and tumble world of packaged goods sales. At Procter & Gamble, you're promised that you'll never work for a boss who hasn't done your job. So she thought, "Oh well, the better I do it, the faster I won't do it." In two years she was promoted to management.

But Connie soon realized the gritty underside of corporate success: the punishing pace of promotion. Back and forth she shuttled, from Milwaukee to Cincinnati to Chicago, and wherever else her bosses needed her to go. All the while, she embraced the corporate world and was a good soldier continuing to move wherever and whenever asked. Until one day she realized she didn't have to keep up the pace anymore.

■ Starting from Scratch

This is not a rags-to-riches story. And it's not a hit-the-ball-out-of-the-park story either; Connie was no Sam Walton. Instead, Connie's rise through corporate America and into entrepreneurship is the kind of thing a lot of high achievers can aspire to. It's not that corporate life is so bad; it's just that in most corporate jobs you don't have a lot of control over how much money you make or where you're going to live.

For Connie, her start as an entrepreneur began as a quiet "inner grumbling" of dissatisfaction when she was promoted to management. The problem was that she was extremely hardworking and gave her job everything she had. What bothered her was that even though she made a decent salary, she realized that her pay was never going to be linked to her effort. Instead, the corporate pay scale is mostly based on how many years you've been with the company—a familiar frustration for many.

By age 35, Connie was making a low six-figure salary as sales manager at S.C. Johnson, where she worked with five different brands, 30 various marketing people, and a 400-member sales team. Between boredom and the money issue, Connie's inner rumblings grew. She tried working at a Chicago consulting firm, but even that was disappointing. When she was ready to quit, her boss at the consulting firm talked her into staying on part-time for a full-time salary—it ended up being the start of a six-month journey to figure out her next move.

Searching for answers, Connie hit the career and self-help book sections of the bookstores and started doing informational interviews. She would call people—even people she didn't know—who worked in careers that she found interesting. She would invite them to lunch or out for coffee and earnestly ask them what they liked about their jobs. She considered working for a not-for-profit, becoming a commodities trader, or fundraising for a charitable foundation. But none of those really seemed right.

Then, one Sunday morning she was lying on the couch reading the Sunday paper and grabbed the real estate section first. "I realized I'd been doing this for years," Connie says. A school friend reminded her that she used to joke about buying rental property; and back in college she used to hang out with architecture students. She had repressed all these desires—but no more. Connie finally realized what she really wanted to do: sell residential real estate. Like many occupations that don't require a college degree (and even some that do), there's a stigma to being a residential Realtor. To be honest, the image problem was the main reason Connie never considered real estate. But it fit.

■ Underestimating Obstacles

Once she'd decided she wanted to be a Realtor, Connie moved quickly. She checked the Internet for information about becoming a licensed real estate agent. Then she did some more informational interviews. She talked to three real estate agents, asking them for advice. They said be prepared for six months with no income; but since she was still drawing a full-time salary (and working part-time), that wasn't really an issue for her.

Connie signed up for a ten-week licensing class that met once a week in the evenings. She learned about title searches, legal terminology, real estate laws, case studies, and a lot of new concepts. During the days, she worked at her sales and marketing consulting job. After work, she would study and dream about her new career. While the classes were helpful, Connie noticed something was missing: the classes offered no practical advice on how to get clients, how to sell houses, or the day-to-day realities of being a Realtor.

So while she was studying, Connie would also talk to people about the ins and outs of residential real estate. She went through all her social and business contacts and called anyone who could help. What she came up with was a contractor, a builder, and an appraiser who gave her a glimpse into Chicago's residential real estate industry. What they told her was that she was facing a crowded field. Real estate agents are a dime a dozen in most big cities.

Meanwhile, Connie passed her class exam and the Illinois real estate licensing exam. Two months after deciding to be a Realtor, she had her real estate license. Now she needed a place to hang her shingle.

The biggest, most prestigious residential real estate firm in Chicago didn't take new agents, so Connie went to work for a smaller firm run by two real estate developers. She hoped to learn the development world from them but was disappointed. In reality, she was just a cash cow for them. Looking back, she wishes she'd been more picky about who she worked for in the beginning. "Remember," she says, "brokers need agents and they will court you." Agents can even negotiate the starting commission, which is the split of the sales commission between Realtor and broker. Connie advises people to set up interviews with three real estate offices where they'd like to work and go with the one that will teach them the most about the business.

When it comes to Connie's first deal, she calls it a "baptism by fire." The client was one of her own neighbors, a couple who wanted to sell their home because the area was becoming gentrified. Despite her lack of experience, the couple trusted her. It was a challenge: they weren't business savvy, the house was in disrepair, and they even owed back taxes. Connie so wanted that first listing that she actually went to the courthouse and paid their back taxes for them (and had them sign a notarized IOU note). After it sold, the buyer, who was a developer, learned his builder went bankrupt and decided to cancel the project. Within six weeks, the house was listed for sale again—and Connie was the selling agent. She earned two sales commissions out of the listing. Connie was on her way.

Her worst moment came when her broker referred a young couple looking for their first home. They decided on a new development just being built. All was well until the developer went belly up. When they finally got back their deposit, the couple decided not to buy a house after all and never called Connie back. "To me, that's a failure," Connie says. Even though she had no way of knowing about the developer's cash problems, she felt horrible about hooking them up with him and resolved to be more thorough about checking out developers.

■ Building Momentum

Connie made some valuable friends in her first months as a Realtor. One of these contacts was the developer who had bought and later sold that first house. He ended up giving her two more listings for other properties that he owned. Another valuable business contact came even before she passed her Realtor's exam; while doing some informational interviewing, she met a real estate appraiser and contractor who she spoke with to get an idea of the Chicago market. Impressed with her drive, a friendship sprung up and he started referring buyers to her.

In her first few months, Connie gathered momentum. Even though she was prepared to go six months without a commission check, she didn't have to. She credits her natural networking ability and the way she's willing to bend over backward to make a deal work. If you don't have a lot of connections, she recommends attending networking events; every city's business newspapers are full of these kinds of events put on by chambers of commerce and charitable groups.

In the real estate world, there's a saying: "Listers last." It means that if you have the capacity to list a house and represent sellers, then your career is more stable. In the residential real estate business, representing buyers—driving them around to look at houses—is the kind of job that doesn't always end up with a commission. People change their minds and don't end up buying. But when a Realtor is on the selling end, eventually the house will sell and the Realtor will get a commission. While Connie also represents buyers, she has set up her business model so that she mostly lists sellers. Thanks to her tireless networking and extra service, most of the time she can laugh.

But even a top producer like Connie has tremendous swings in cash flow. You can have a year that starts out great in the first six months but then yields nothing over the fall and winter months, which are generally slow in Chicago's market. "If you don't plan, you could be screwed," Connie says. The longest gap she had between commission checks was three and a half months, but she knows someone who is going on five months. "There are no guarantees," she says.

To keep momentum going, Connie goes above and beyond the call of duty. Recently, a friend referred a federal employee moving to Chicago from Washington, D.C., who was looking to buy a house. She spent some time with him on the phone, talking about what kind of home he was looking for. The next day he called to apologize. Unknown to him, his wife had gone out and simultaneously interviewed another real estate agent. The couple decided to go with the other agent because he worked with the government relocation program and they would get a $1,000 incentive. "I very graciously said, 'If it doesn't work out or you need any help, don't hesitate to call; you're a friend of my friend.' I let it pass." She got a phone call six weeks later from the couple, saying the Realtor had taken them on two disastrous house-hunting trips. They asked, "We were wondering if you had time to work with us or did we burn that bridge?" She ended up finding them a home and they subsequently referred four other government employees who relocated to Chicago and bought homes through her.

In any fight, it's the guy who's willing to die who will win the inch. When Connie became a real estate agent, she fought hard. All the sales and marketing skills she'd learned in corporate jobs clicked in.

When she runs an open house, Connie spends her own money to supply giveaways to attract traffic. Whether it's a bottle of wine, a retail gift certificate, or a catered luncheon—nothing is too good for her prospective clients. And if she has an unusual, upscale property that deserves national attention, Connie will pay for an ad in the *Wall Street Journal* out of her own pocket. Anything to get the best price for her seller.

■ Taking the Next Leap

Higher selling prices mean higher commission checks. Once Connie was established, she started going for the high end: expensive homes edging up into the million-dollar range. And that means working with more demanding clients. She found this out when she went for her first million-dollar listing. When she met the sellers, Connie was gracious and businesslike; she was sure they would choose her. But they didn't. So Connie did something that we can all learn from: she called and asked why. "They said they figured my small firm didn't have the tools to market a million-dollar home," Connie recalls. So she moved to a bigger firm.

In 2004, Connie reached $10 million in sales. She plans to double that in 2005. But now that she's at the top of her game, Connie is taking another look inside and deciding to slow down. She realized she needed to do this when a broker congratulated her for her record sales, and she confessed she was disappointed because she was number seven out of 150 agents at the firm. Then the broker pointed out to her that all the Realtors above her worked with partners; it dawned on Connie that maybe she was single-handedly doing the workload of two people.

So Connie made another leap: she hired an assistant in 2005. That spring was the first time she'd taken a Saturday off in the lucrative spring market.

Connie admits her job can be stressful because the biggest investment many people make is their home. How long it takes to sell a home and what kind of price she's able to get is so important to her clients. "I can't be cavalier; I have to protect their interests," Connie says. "I take on people's stuff, and I'm exhausted by the end of the day."

But her job is also exhilarating. For example, one of her biggest deals lately was what Realtors call a "teardown," where the land is worth far more than the house. This particular property was a ramshackle house sitting on beachfront property on the south side of Chicago. "In essence, I was selling dirt on the beach," Connie says. Using her own money, she marketed the property to the membership of the city's six yacht clubs. In five and a half months, the property sold for $1.5 million. It was an excellent price.

Another thing Connie loves about working for herself as a Realtor is that she feels she's doing something that matters. Connie once told her boss at S.C. Johnson Wax that she didn't want her epitaph to read: "She sold a lot of shit." Although she's still selling something—houses—Connie feels like she's also problem solving. People come to her with a problem: they're making a change in their lives and want her to help them sell their home and find a new one. She guides them through this milestone and gets to see the looks on their faces when they finally have their new home. That's a little more compelling than selling cleaning products.

And Connie loves the money she's making, which is more than she earned in corporate America when she left—and probably more than she'd ever hope to make as a cog in a wheel. Best of all, when it comes to deciding where to live, she'll never have to pick up and move unless she wants to. For Connie, that's something to be thrilled about.

Chapter Six

Warren Brown, Founder of **CakeLove** and **Love Café**

Have a Cause

Warren Brown is simply one of the coolest cats you can ever meet—and he's a man on a mission. A mission to make cake and change the face of sex education across the nation. Sounds to me like a sweet combo with a purpose. By the time we finished our three-hour talk over the best cake in town, my hyper, edge-of-the-seat questioning had downshifted into a state of calm. I began wondering how this guy was going to continue to inspire, educate, and stay on track building an empire around flour, vanilla extract, fresh strawberries, and chocolate ganache.

Warren started his career as a litigator for the federal government, a job that makes him yawn whenever he talks about it. He had envisioned a job where everyone worked hard to fight injustice, taking on doctors who refuse to treat homeless people or hospitals that turn away ambulances because the patient doesn't have health insurance. Instead, he took only one case to court in two years on the job. He was drained and depressed and knew he had to make a change.

Now, as president of the CakeLove bakery and Love Café in Washington, D.C., Warren is still bucking the system. This time, he's fighting the made-from-a-mix status quo with his lovingly made-from-scratch cakes. Real butter and pure vanilla extract may not save the world, but Warren thinks it's worth a try.

Back in his college days at Brown University, Warren never thought of himself as an entrepreneur—but he was a leader and a great public speaker, having learned early the power of the media. When date-rape rumors put the Brown campus on national news, Warren was part of a group that confronted the issue head-on by bringing sexual assault prevention classes to the campus. A great speaker with an easygoing way of talking about hot topics that people would really rather *not* talk about, Warren opened a lot of minds.

It led to jobs teaching sex education and health to high school kids. And it opened Warren's eyes to the world outside his Ivy League upbringing. Most people, he realized, didn't examine the world's problems and try to deal with them. Warren wanted a job where he could shake things up, make a substantive difference, and get people to stop sweeping problems under the rug. Instead of just teaching kids, he wanted to set his sights higher and change the education system itself.

Law school seemed like a logical step, so Warren threw himself into his classes at George Washington law school. One graduate degree is hard enough work for most people, but Warren also earned a master's degree in public health. And in the midst of it all, he had a sneaking feeling that he'd made a career mistake. To deal with the grinding stress, Warren would spend his free hours staying up late to cook amazing gourmet foods and then invite everyone he knew to come over and help eat his creations. "I needed a way to vent," Warren says. It was more then venting. He didn't know it at the time, but those food parties were also planting the seeds for CakeLove.

Only three months into his first job after law school, Warren was sure he'd made a mistake. He'd cut his long, cool dreadlocks to fit in at the federal office he worked in and was working late on a Friday night to research a case that was headed for the U.S. Supreme Court. It was important, exciting stuff. Then he looked around and realized he was alone; all his coworkers were long gone. And here he was, passionately committed to changing the world, in a place where what you wore—a suit and tie—seemed more important than what you did.

At that moment, Warren had a revelation: he'd rather be baking cakes.

■ Starting from Scratch

Even though Warren stuck out his job at the Department of Health and Human Services for another year and a half, he was looking for a way to make cakes his career. On New Year's Eve, 1999, he made the resolution that he would learn everything he needed to make cakes his business.

Somehow, it all made sense. The world would be a better place, Warren figured, if folks felt free to pursue their passions in life. Plus—people were happy when they saw cakes. Warren saw what a cake could do to a crowd. It happened one day when he was still working as a lawyer and was flying from D.C. to New York to visit family. Usually, people at airports do everything they can to avoid eye contact. But not that day. Everyone he passed at least smiled or said "Hi" to Warren. What was the difference? He was carrying a plastic-wrapped homemade chocolate cake on a simple dinner plate. Something about a homemade baked item makes people happy—and happy people make for a better world.

"It was like a people magnet," Warren says, and even though he's told this story a million times, you can still hear the excitement in his voice. After that trip, Warren knew he'd found a way to make the world a better place. I can make this at home, he reasoned, and there are hardly any start-up costs.

One Thursday in late January 2000, Warren started baking. He baked for three days straight. By Sunday, he had 15 cakes ready for his "cake open house." It was a lot like the gourmet food parties he used to have in college, except this time it was a business.

Seventy-five of his friends crowded into his apartment to sample cakes and complete a survey about which ones they liked best. Some of them even placed orders.

There's always a point in an entrepreneur's life when he or she looks back and realizes the exact moment he or she started to take himself or herself seriously. Usually, it comes with that first order. For Warren, he realized CakeLove was more than a dream the moment people started ordering cakes at his party. Before that, Warren had sold only four cakes in his life. Now, in one day, he had presold ten times that and was selling a few cakes a week.

Some of those friends that Warren had made over the years came to help get things off the ground. One came for the weekend with his girlfriend to help bake and clean for the party. Warren's sister made business cards; a lawyer friend helped write up and copy the menu and survey. "We had fun," Warren remembers. "I jumped into it." Then it started to move beyond his circle of friends: by Valentine's Day, he got his first order from someone he didn't know.

The thing about having a cause is that it inspires people. And Warren's cause is about encouraging people to make the world a better place by using their talents. It's the kind of cause that speaks to everyone from any walk of life. Warren at first thought his great personality and intellect would help him with a law career. Now, it turns out, there are a lot of disillusioned lawyers out there who might not have the courage or ability to leave law and become entrepreneurs as Warren did. But those lawyers can live vicariously through Warren's dream by buying his cakes. And they were fast becoming some of Warren's best customers.

But before Warren could make the final leap from his law career, he would land himself in the emergency room.

■ Underestimating Obstacles

Through the busy days of starting his bakery out of his apartment, Warren was still working full-time as an administrative lawyer and moonlighting as a baker. And instead of being a way to relax, baking became a demanding job.

This two-career lifestyle came crashing down in one memorable, sleepless weekend. It started with a weekend retreat for his federal job. After the grueling weekend, he had a two-hour drive from West Virginia to his apartment, where he dropped his bags and went to work for three hours making cakes into the night. Then he got up early, delivered the cakes, went to work for a full day at the federal prosecutors office, and then drove to an evening wedding—where they were serving his cake. By Tuesday night, he was on the phone with his father, a doctor, who told him to go to the emergency room. That's where Warren got his diagnosis: exhaustion. His doctor told the 29-year-old to slow down: "You're not 15 anymore."

Cooking and baking were always Warren's way to blow off steam and relax. In the kitchen, he could totally immerse himself in the task at hand and in the smells and textures of food. He could also be creative and throw in a dash of ground almonds if the spirit moved him or arrange orange slices in a flower-petal pattern on a cake. Afterward, he'd watch the smiles on people's faces as they enjoyed his food. When the doctor told Warren to slow down, he knew in his bones that baking was not the reason he was exhausted. The problem was his law career.

Like Maria Churchill in Chapter 1, Warren was trying to make a business out of a hobby. But unlike her, he didn't have the push of a layoff to launch him on that path. For him, the emergency room visit was the push.

Looking back, leaving law was obviously the right decision. But back then it wasn't so clear. Warren had spent three years slaving at classes for his law degree, plus he'd studied and passed the New York State bar exam, one of the hardest in the nation. Even though he was only in his late 20s, Warren had achieved a lot with his law career. Yet his heart just wasn't in it. No matter what people thought, ending up in the emergency room taught Warren he had to choose. He chose CakeLove.

Even though he was an extremely smart guy, Warren knew he wasn't going to change the world as a lawyer. During his days at the office, he felt himself turning cynical when he confronted lawyers who split hairs over whether a hospital had a legal responsibility to help an indigent woman in labor if she was standing on the curb at the emergency room asking for help. It made him sick to hear the legalistic arguments—"Just talk to me, man," Warren wanted to scream. "I mean, there are people in crisis and the lawyers are fighting over whether their toes were over the curb."

Even though he was barely getting enough cake orders to get by, Warren took a two-month leave of absence from work and set out to do things right. He got an appointment with a community development office and asked for advice; they hooked him up with a building owner who had a little hole-in-the-wall commercial kitchen he could sublease. Even though it wasn't the sunny, open bakery Warren had in mind, it would do just fine.

■ Building Momentum

On the second day of his leave of absence, something happened that would change Warren's life. He met a *Washington Post* food section reporter who wanted to try some of his cakes. When she heard his personal story about leaving his law career to be a baker, the reporter said she wanted to keep in touch and follow him through the process and then write about it. "Great, write about me now; I need the publicity!" Warren said. Knowing that newspapers generally aren't in the business of offering free publicity, Warren nevertheless kept in touch with the reporter as he went through the process of buying equipment and signing a lease for the little commercial kitchen he was using.

After the leave was over, Warren quit law for good. At that point, he was selling just enough cakes to pay the rent and using savings and credit cards for everything else. For a year and a half he went on that way. "I was running out of money," he recalls. "I didn't have enough capital. I would have sunk without those credit cards."

Just before momentum catches on, many entrepreneurs talk about reaching a point where they're not sure they will make it. That's because even a great hunter runs out of resources. Some find relief in bankruptcy court. For Warren, help came from the *Washington Post*, which finally came out with its article about the struggles of a lawyer trying to break out of the rigid mold of his career.

"That story changed my life," recalls Warren, whose face ran on the front cover of *Washington Post*'s prestigious food section. "It was huge. The phones were ringing for two days." One of those calls was from *People* magazine; another was from Oprah. Getting an endorsement from Oprah with national television exposure is a lightning rod for business. Warren appreciated the interest and gave great interviews, charming viewers with his passionate drive. Sales jumped 400 percent in just a few months.

In the midst of the attention, Warren took out a $125,000 loan (backed by the Small Business Administration) and opened his first storefront bakery. It was small—only 600 square feet—but it had a big picture window out front where he could watch passersby on D.C.'s bustling U Street corridor. Sometimes, with the heat of the ovens and the constant stream of customers, Warren feels like he's in a clothes dryer on the high tumble-dry setting. But he's happier than he's ever been—and he's making as much as he would have if he'd remained a federal litigator. Plus, his business and brand are fast becoming an asset.

Best of all, Warren loves the way his bakery makes him feel. Like all of the entrepreneurs in this book, Warren says a bad day at a business you love is better than your best day in a so-so job working for someone else. At CakeLove, he makes the rules. Sometimes, he knows he's being a stickler, insisting on making cakes from scratch, using only unbleached flour and butter—never the bleached flour and hydrogenated shortening that are the staples at most American bakeries nowadays. But his high standards are congruent with his mission to make a better cake.

He talks to people about using wholesome ingredients and encourages them to try baking from scratch in their own homes. Sure, he says, baking can be a little intimidating because it depends on precise measurements and chemical reactions. But even though there's some science to it, baking is an art. And he wants people to enjoy life to the fullest and reach inside and find their talents.

To Warren, mixing their own cake from scratch is a way for people to take off their blinders and explore the world around them. His customers love it. They like to hang around and chat with him about it. And Warren loves it too. With all his media exposure, folks feel they know Warren, and they call him up from all over the country to talk about how they want to follow their passion but are afraid to quit their jobs. Warren and his cakes inspire them.

■ Taking the Next Leap

In late 2002, Warren expanded into the Love Café, a little restaurant with a light breakfast and lunch menu that serves dessert and espresso all day long. A year later, he did something very important: he started staying away from the bakery and café.

That's because as much as Warren loves to bake, he's serious about building a business and not just having a job. That's an insight that can take a long time for an entrepreneur to realize. Warren learned it early on, almost by accident, when the media storm hit and he quickly opened his first storefront. The problem was that before opening the storefront he'd already had a vacation planned. After working for nearly two years without time off, it was a well-earned vacation that he'd planned for months. His brush with overworking taught him that everyone, even a busy entrepreneur, needs some time off.

While he was away, Warren's employees had to run the store. It didn't go without a hitch or two, but the place also didn't burn down. By taking time off when things were rolling, he taught himself and the staff a valuable lesson: the staff is entrusted with the important job of running the bakery, not just doing what Warren tells them to do.

He and his staff have weathered other storms, like the downturn after September 11. Luckily, CakeLove had just finished it's busy wedding cake season and had enough money in the bank to keep afloat.

The Atkins diet craze, which started in late 2003, also hurt profits into 2004, even during the usually busy winter holiday season. At one point, profits dropped 30 percent. Warren didn't jump on the low-carb bandwagon. His philosophy is that cake is not a diet food; it's a treat. He even copyrighted the phrase "Nothing is fat free" and features that slogan on his menus.

Sure enough, sales were back up in 2005, which was good because Warren's expenses had been going up. For example, dairy prices nearly doubled during his first year of business. Dairy farmers, it turns out, were seeing a worldwide demand increase for milk and were able to pass on higher prices to the consumer. Great news for the dairy farmer but bad for the price of butter, a vital ingredient in CakeLove cakes.

Ups and downs are a fact of life in business, and Warren is busy hunting for the next opportunity. For one thing, he plans on opening more storefronts in the D.C. suburbs. For another, he's developing a candy bar sweetened with honey—and maybe an energy bar. Something with a longer shelf life than cake, so it could be mass distributed.

In just six years, Warren went from being an unhappy lawyer to a happy entrepreneur. Warren can lead his cause, and have his cake and eat it too.

PART 2

Underestimate Your Obstacles ■

"A pessimist sees the difficulty in every opportunity; an optimist sees the opportunity in every difficulty." Winston Churchill said this during World War II when London was being bombarded by the Germans. The situation looked hopeless, but Churchill had an invincible vision of winning the war.

The first part of the HUNT is a very internal process: figuring out what you're good at and what you love and discovering your personal strenqths. When you go through the H step of the HUNT and harness what you have, you create a vision. The HUNT's second step, Underestimating Your Obstacles, focuses on protecting and strengthening that vision. Instead of seeing obstacles as something that will destroy what you have or roadblocks along the way, look at obstacles as tools to hone your vision. Analyze your goal with a focus on how you can nurture it and make it work rather than on all the ways it can go wrong. For example, the optimist who wants to start his own widget business realizes his obstacle is navigating the details. So he talks to trademark lawyers and widget manufacturers who will help bring his vision into reality. An optimist doesn't get bogged down with the complicated regulations of the U.S. widget industry.

We're not all born optimists. And we're not all raised that way. (Some of the funniest people I know are natural-born cynics and pessimists.) But if you're going to be in business and be an entrepreneur, you have to focus optimistically on your vision and not let the thousand things that can go wrong stand in the way. When you HUNT, you need to keep your destination on the horizon at all times.

Many people mistakenly think that their biggest stumbling block is lack of knowledge. Time and time again, I hear people say they don't have enough expertise or experience to start a business. They say: "I can't start a new bakery because I don't know enough about baking." "I can't get involved in real estate because I don't know enough about houses." "I can't start a software company because I don't know anything about computers." "I can't start a mortgage business because I don't know enough about lending and finance." Well, guess what? No entrepreneur has all the skills necessary to make his or her vision a reality.

In this book, you'll find that almost none of the entrepreneurs I talked with had major experience in the business that they started from scratch. They had general skills, but they didn't necessarily have industry-specific expertise. That's part of the reason I named the book *Starting from Scratch*. If you lack experience in a certain business sector, partner with or hire someone who does. Or work in your target industry for a year or so to learn the ropes.

Another stumbling block people worry about is *competition*. Hunting in the business world is competitive work. In this day and age, any individual has hundreds of thousands of competitors all going after the same thing. The successful person has a vision that looks at the competition and says "I can do better." By all means, don't underestimate your competition, but do underestimate your obstacles to being better than your competition. Don't waste your vision because you feel as though you can't compete. Instead, refine your vision so it's better and fresher than your competitors'.

One way to get better at underestimating obstacles is by following the example of others. If you listen to the outcome of stories where people truly underestimated obstacles, you'll realize that almost anything you can envision is achievable. Every single person in this book got to their goal by underestimating obstacles. And there are several examples that are more striking than others.

These next five stories of ordinary people show five different ways of underestimating obstacles:

- **Secrecy.** This worked for Sara Blakely. She realized that everyone was going to have an opinion about her idea for a new kind of pantyhose, especially her highly educated MBA friends. So she didn't tell them. In this way, she avoided learning that the U.S. hosiery business was dying. Since she didn't know about this significant obstacle she freed up her energy to create her own hosiery brand. That doesn't mean she was naïve; Sara was careful to file a trademark for her new hosiery idea and harnessed her sales expertise to deal with cheap foreign competitors.
- **Be unconventional.** Jon Shibley turned the traditional mortgage business model on its ear. He didn't worry that the largest mortgage lenders in the country might not want to consider his new business model. Instead, Jon worked at putting himself in a position of power so the mortgage lenders would have to listen.
- **Keep it weird.** Steve Bercu found that when it came to running an independent bookstore, different was better. Instead of giving up market share to national chains, he breathed new life into a failing

bookstore, rejuvenated himself, and became a minor celebrity in his community.

- **Work the system.** Alan Thompson had to work the kinks out of his business plan until he finally tweaked it into the right shape. Once he had his system perfected, he was able to sell it to others.

- **Resiliency.** Faced with natural disasters and unbelievable back luck, including a ruined brand-new shipment of fireworks, David York had the fortitude to stick to his vision, get a new storehouse, order more inventory, and begin again. He kept this spirit throughout his career, overcoming numerous setbacks.

Obstacles are a gift. Obstacles tell you what you need to do to shore up your vision. They are hurdles, not barriers. Don't give away your power: When you hit an obstacle, cut right through it, ignore it, blast it aside, or go right around it. Use it as an opportunity to strengthen and clarify your vision, but never let it stop you. Just get on with your hunt. If you're not doing this, learn from people who have, learn the U step of the HUNT, and keep reading.

▪ Chapter Seven

Sara Blakely, Founder of **Spanx**

Keep It a Secret

Sara Blakely and I had both lived in Atlanta for more than six years, yet we never ran into one another until our paths crossed in the most unlikely of places: QVC headquarters, in West Chester, Pennsylvania. I was selling the Delonge Panini Grill, and she was selling Spanx to the world. Now, I'm back to my day job as a financial advisor, and she's still selling high-end women's undergarment fashion and helping women—from Oprah and Gwyneth Paltrow to my mother in Pennsylvania—to make their panty lines disappear.

Back in the day—when she was desperate to get out of selling fax machines for a living—Sara Blakely kept her start-up a secret for more than a year and then launched it from secret to sensation in six weeks.

While networking is a great way to bootstrap, Sara's story shows that sometimes the best thing for your great business idea is to keep it a secret between you, your lawyer, and your manufacturer. When she built a business around a new kind of body-shaper for women, secrecy was part of her winning formula.

"Don't tell anyone, not even your friends and family," advises Sara, who gets thousands of e-mails a year from women asking for advice on how to start garment businesses. When she finally unveiled her body-shaper underwear, it skyrocketed to the top, winning Oprah's coveted "Favorite Things" endorsement within just six weeks. By the time she told friends and family, she was beyond caring whether people thought it was a good idea. "Wait until you've invested enough of yourself in it that you won't turn back," she says. "If you really believe in your idea and it works for you, that's enough. I didn't need a focus group to see my butt in my pants."

Sara knew people might snicker about her product, designed to change women's lives by eliminating panty lines forever. Even her company name, Spanx, sounded like the punch line from a stand-up comic's act. In fact, she'd dabbled in stand-up comedy—and she knew the power of words and first impressions. Her gut told her to keep it to herself so she wouldn't be discouraged by what people might say about her. There she was, with no background in the garment industry, staking her savings on producing a line of ladies undergarments. So she gently put off questions with a mysterious smile. "All they knew was 'Sara has an invention.' They all laughed about it: 'Last week it was being a comedian, now she's inventing something.'"

Her family is close, her friends supportive. Sara just wasn't the sort of person people pegged as the owner of a multi-million-dollar company. Plus, her idea was so simple. "The minute you put your idea out there you have to defend it and explain it," she says. "It can really stop someone in that infant stage of an idea. You won't believe how many people tell me they've had great ideas for businesses but often got the response, 'If it's such a great idea, then why isn't anyone doing it already?'" The point, she says, is to look for the business potential behind everyday ideas.

■ Starting from Scratch

Sara believes in visualizing what she wants. Each day before she went out to sell fax machines and train salespeople, Sara would think about how nice it would be to have a product of her own to sell. As she drove to work in Atlanta traffic, she would say to herself, "I want my idea; I'm ready for it."

Whatever the idea turned out to be, Sara knew she could sell it. She yearned for a product with mass appeal—not like faxes and copiers that only interested office-supply people. If she could combine her talent for sales with a product that she really loved, Sara knew the sky would be the limit.

Success in business was something Sara hungered for, even as a child. Weekends she would think up ways to make money: a roller skating rink in her playroom, a putt-putt golf course in the yard, selling her old toys or drawings door-to-door, and even sewing charms on socks and selling them to schoolmates. In high school, she passed out flyers promoting her babysitting service to families on the beach near her St. Petersburg home. She made several hundred dollars a day just hanging out in her bathing suit entertaining little kids on the beach. She made more money in two months during the summer than any of her friends did throughout the year.

But Sara had also known failure. As a child, she'd yearned to be a lawyer like her father. She'd even gotten out of school to listen to his closing argument on a case. But her dream of being a lawyer shattered when she couldn't pass the law school entrance exams. She'd gotten over losing that dream, but she wasn't going to lose any more.

When her idea came to her in 1998, Sara was ready. It happened as she was dressing for a party. Just before she left home, she checked out her rear view in the mirror and gasped. Visible panty lines. Or, as she now calls them, VPLs. She scrounged through her drawers, looking for something to wear under her new cream pants. "I was so frustrated. What are women really supposed to wear under white pants?" she recalls. Her solution to the underwear crisis was to cut off the feet of her control top pantyhose and wear them underneath the cream pants.

It turns out this isn't such an original idea. It was the first time Sara had resorted to cutting apart pantyhose, but apparently women have been doing this for a while. Who knew? Women come up to her all the time now and say, "Sara, I've been cutting the feet out of my pantyhose for 20 years; why didn't I invent this?"

The answer is that Sara saw the business potential because she had an entrepreneurial mind-set. She was hunting for a way out of an exhausting sales job. In this opportunistic frame of mind she was mentally ready to find a new product and take it to market. All it took was cutting the feet off of her pantyhose *once* and she saw the potential. For some women, the undergarment solution was just a way to finish off an outfit. For Sara, it was a sign from the universe. And she was more willing than the average person to take risks in pursuit of rewards. Here was the product Sara had wished for. She wasn't going to squander the opportunity.

First she needed a name. Since Coca-Cola and Kodak are the most recognized brands in the world, Sara figured she needed a *k* sound in the name. Also, from doing stand-up comedy, she knew that the *k* sound makes people laugh. Mulling over *k* sounds, the slightly naughty *spanks* came to mind. Then she changed the *ks* to *x* when she found out that made-up words are easier to trademark. That's how Spanx came to be.

Next, from her work in sales Sara knew she needed a prototype of her Spanx garment to show to department store buyers—but that meant sharing the secret with someone. So Sara read a book on inventions and found out that in the business world there's a formal way to keep a secret: a nondisclosure agreement. Based on one she saw in a book, Sara wrote up her own nondisclosure agreement and sent it to the product development departments of more than 15 hosiery mills that she'd found on the Internet. In the letter, she described her footless pantyhose garment and asked them to quote her a price for manufacturing a prototype. Then she waited for their answers.

◼ Underestimating Obstacles

When the hosiery mills replied, they were brutally honest. They all thought the idea was stupid or didn't make sense. They also wanted to know who she was. Who were her backers? Was she representing a larger company? When they realized it was just Sara with her life savings of $5,000, the mills backed off.

But Sara was used to refusals. She even knew what it was like to have her business card ripped up in her face by receptionists when she went around peddling fax machines. So she pushed ahead and called three patent lawyers, who quoted her the price of $3,000 to $5,000 to write her patent. That would eat up all her savings. So she read up about patents and found out the most costly part is the search, which means looking through all the patents ever registered to be sure that no one already patented something similar. She bargained with the attorneys: "How about if I write the entire package except for the claims? Will you give me a discount?" In the end, she found one attorney who just plain felt sorry for her and wrote the claims portion of the patent for just $700.

To search all the registered patents, Sara set out each day after work to the Georgia Institute of Technology library. There she spent hours going over patents all the way back to the 1800s. The search took the better part of a year. But she did it, along with some help with a book about patents and trademarks.

Still, when the mills weren't budging, Sara needed encouragement. She told herself that if her business were meant to be, she would get a sign. And then, part prayer, part wish, she asked the universe for a sign: "I'm either supposed to do this or not; let me know." Two months later she got her sign. Sara had just done a sales seminar and headed to her hotel room and clicked on the TV to the *Oprah* show. There was Oprah, lifting her pant leg and showing the world she had cut the feet off her pantyhose to solve an undergarment issue. For Sara, that was her sign.

She jumped up off the bed in her hotel room and said: "No matter what, I'm not stopping!" She took a week off work, called the mills that had turned her down, and said, "I'm coming—in person." She showed them her footless pantyhose and some pieces of stretch lace from craft stores. Once again, they all sent her away.

Hosiery, it turns out, is a volume commodity. To change production slows down the machines; it would cost the mills money to experiment with her idea. No one wanted to take a risk on a 27-year-old with $5,000 and a dream. Two weeks later, one mill owner called her back. She was glad he called her back but wondered why the change of heart. He said he had two daughters, and both admitted they had cut the feet off their pantyhose to create an undergarment just like Sara's prototype. Since Sara was fussy about her shaper, she turned down a couple of the mill's first attempts—and because her project was not high priority, it took eight months to get the prototype for Spanx made exactly as she wanted it.

It was a good thing Sara kept her idea from friends. If she had told them, she might have found out that the obstacles were even worse than she knew. Hosiery has been considered a dying industry for the past 15 years, thanks to cheap foreign imports. It's virtually unheard of to start a new hosiery brand nowadays.

Keeping her idea secret also kept her from getting advice on the typical way to drum up interest in a new garment: go to a trade show. Getting noticed at trade shows is a route that usually takes years. If she'd known about trade shows, she might have set up her table next to 50 other hopefuls and been overlooked. Instead, she planned on using her old sales technique to cold-call department stores. Sara didn't know she was going against protocol, but that paid off for her.

Even her label went against tradition. Sara bought ten packages of pantyhose, laid them out on the floor, and critiqued the labels—all were boring. So she had an artist design a bright-red package with three cartoon women on the front. Also, since she had no idea what legally needed to be on the package, she just compared the other packages and whatever they mentioned on their labels—fabric content, country of origin, and so on—she put on her label. After her mom said it wasn't too naughty, she also added her tagline: "Don't worry, we've got your butt covered!"

■ Building Momentum

As Sara set out to unveil her product to department stores, the U.S. Patent and Trademark Office, and the world, she had an attack of nerves. Something wasn't right.

The problem was in the listing of fibers that made up her garment. Sara had gotten the fabric content directly from one of the workers at the hosiery mill. In his heavy North Carolina accent, the mill worker dictated the fabric content: mainly nylon and lacquer. Sara had typed this all up herself. But the night before she submitted her patent, she knew in her gut that something wasn't right. "How can there be lacquer in this?" she asked herself. The next day, she called back the mill worker and asked him to spell *lacquer*. It turned out *lacquer* was really *lycra*. Sara called her patent attorney and did a quick correction.

Sara was such a newcomer to the garment industry that she didn't even know how to go about approaching a department store. So with her prototype in hand in its bright-red package, she did what she would have done selling a fax machine: she just called the nearest Neiman Marcus store out of her local phone book. Whoever answered the phone told her to call company headquarters in Dallas. She called Dallas and simply said she had a product that will "change your customers' lives." Then Sara hopped on a plane. She took along her cream pants, the ones that had started it all nearly two years before. Face-to-face with the Neiman Marcus buyer, Sara took the buyer into the ladies room, where she modeled the cream pants with the Spanx and without. That sold it.

Within five minutes of showing the prototype Spanx, the buyer ordered several thousand pairs to test at seven stores. It was brilliant. Even the hosiery mill owner was surprised to get the manufacturing order for a test run of 7,000 pairs of Spanx for Neiman Marcus. When Sara called the mill owner with the good news, there was dead silence on the other end. He'd thought he would never hear from her again.

Sara had also begun letting out the secret to friends and family. Once she had a prototype and orders from Neiman Marcus, she called everyone she knew in the seven cities that Neiman Marcus was testing. "If you go into the store and make a big deal about this product and buy it, I'll mail you a check for $20," Sara told them. When the large sizes weren't selling, Sara drove her own brother to a Neiman Marcus store and sent him inside to make a big deal about Spanx and buy up the big sizes.

She also started spreading the word to buyers at Saks. As she continued her grassroots campaign, she got a call from the Neiman Marcus buyer, saying, "You're never going to believe this; we've sold out of the product." Sara believed it. This was the idea she had hoped for and nurtured for all those years. Now everyone was going to know about Spanx.

■ Taking the Next Leap

To really get the ball rolling, Sara made an incredibly smart move. She sent Oprah a gift basket of Spanx with a note explaining how her show had helped in her moment of need. "You were part of my sign," she wrote. "This is my product; it's selling at Neiman Marcus. I want you to have this and I want to get on your show."

Just that simple gift basket and heartfelt note was the trick that got her noticed. Within six weeks, she got on Oprah's list of "Favorite Things." It just goes to show that you might as well start out reaching for the stars.

From that point, life and business snowballed. Spanx has grown faster than Sara ever could have imagined. Even more interesting, Sara's never spent a dime on advertising. She has in-house PR, which is extremely effective and worth millions to her. Another brilliant move was Sara's feat in getting on Richard Branson's reality show, *The Rebel Billionaire,* where she was able to talk about Spanx twice for 15 minutes on national TV. That kind of television exposure and celebrity endorsement are priceless.

Another thing about Sara's business sense—just like landing Oprah's and Richard Branson's shows—she has an uncanny ability to start at the top. She did the same by knocking on the doors of top, high-end retailers. "I know if you start at the high end it's always easier to go down," she says. "But once you start in the middle market it's almost impossible to go up."

Starting with high-end retailers also helped Sara hold on to her customers when cheaper copies of Spanx came into the market. At Neiman Marcus, her brand captured affluent customers, who generally have the most brand loyalty. Sure enough, within six months of launching Spanx, everyone knocked off her signature footless pantyhose and underpriced her. Sara didn't fight the billion-dollar companies for trademark infringement. That would have cost hundreds of thousands of dollars even if she won. In Sara's mind, filing a patent was mainly to make sure that she wasn't vulnerable to lawsuits. Her hunch was good: gradually, many of the knockoffs have come and gone.

Her advice to other start-ups is to put what little money you have into the effort of being first to market. And have a clever name. A patent is important, but don't blow your entire budget on attorney fees to get one.

Where is Sara going next? She is building up the company, trying to stay ahead of the competition by coming up with new products. She now has a line of 40 products, including her signature footless pantyhose, maternity footless hose, bandless trouser socks, stretchy half-slips, and even an aromatherapy lingerie detergent.

The past four years have been an unbelievable ride. She was awarded the Ernst & Young Entrepreneur of the Year Award in 2002, and she was voted Woman of the Year in 2005 for the state of Georgia. Right now, she's dreaming about how nice it would be to be on the cover of *Time* magazine. With her drive and enthusiasm, who knows?

Sara's advice to other start-ups: "Go within yourself and ask what makes sense. Don't ask friends or family for their advice right away. Listen to your own gut instincts and map out a sensible strategy. Don't worry so much about what other people know or think they know." If she had known everything about the hosiery market, Spanx may not even exist.

Sara kept her secret. For a while, at least. And now—she's a sensation.

Chapter Eight

Jon Shibley, Founder of **Lenox Financial Mortgage**   ■

Embrace the Unconventional

Jon Shibley does windows. He also does no-closing-cost mortgages, plays the guitar, and is famous for the most outrageously down-to-earth radio ads in the history of the world! He's a legend in the mortgage business and is known all over the South for his unconventional antics. He has turned the mortgage industry upside down with his company, Lenox Financial Mortgage, but that story comes a little later.

Mainly, Jon Shibley is convinced that he can find a better way to do things, and that doesn't always make people happy. But it has made Jon—and the people who work for him—very successful. "I kind of play the world of business like you'd play a couple hands of poker," says Jon, using his Texas drawl to emphasize just how much of a maverick he is.

Take the window-washing business he started in college, for example. It flew in the face of what he calls America's number one motto: "We don't do windows." Well, Jon's company did do windows. He hired fellow students at Texas Christian University to get up on ladders and clean windows in swanky neighborhoods; a crew could do one house in about two hours, especially when he paid workers $10 per hour—an excellent rate for manual labor in the early 1990s. With that pay, workers had a pretty good incentive to work quickly and leave crystal clear panes.

"I'd get the guys working, then I'd go knock on other doors in the neighborhood and say, 'Hey, we're doing the Smith's house over here, how about you?'" recalls Jon, who says he got very few no answers. "If you try exclusive neighborhoods, there's no woman who will say no to having her windows cleaned. And no husband is ever going to say no to having the windows cleaned because he's afraid he'll have to do it himself."

Jon stumbled onto his unconventional philosophy early on: Do something no one else does and hire a well-paid team to make it happen.

■ Starting from Scratch

Even though the window-washing business earned him $70,000 a year—and expanded into general contracting for home repairs— Jon sold the business after graduation from college in the early 1990s and took a year off to figure out what to do with the rest of his life. While he was in college, as a valet he had parked a few cars, including the car of Texas billionaire Richard Rainwater. Later, he wrote a letter to Rainwater, letting him know he'd parked his Ferrari and that everything was smooth until about 8,000 RPMs—I'm sure that got his attention. And Jon told Rainwater he admired his career and would do an internship for free. Incredibly, the brash note worked, and Rainwater agreed to meet and discuss the offer. Jon ended up getting the job and for the brief period he worked for Rainwater he was able to learn the commercial real estate business from a billionaire. Sound familiar?

He learned from Rainwater: "If you're going to invest in anything, don't do it unless the partners in the deal have a superstar track record," Jon recalls. "Go with the team, not the concept."

For Jon, that meant that he would invest in his own "elite team"; he just had to find a product or service for them to sell. He studied business situations with a technique he'd perfected in college: disregard the rules. Rather than go to class, since Texas Christian University didn't have attendance requirements, he spent class time in the library breaking down his textbooks chapter-by-chapter and then quizzing himself. In Jon's first semester, when he actually attended classes, his grades averaged a dismal 1.3 out of a possible 4.0. "I went to a 3.5 the next semester doing it my way," he says.

That lesson sent him looking at the business world with the attitude that he would learn an industry inside out. Then he would figure out a way to turn it on its head.

First off, he focused on choosing a location. He was attracted to Atlanta because of its gorgeous women, Southern charm, and an explosive growing real estate market. Fortune 500 companies were flocking to the city, setting up headquarters, and sending population figures soaring. Very quickly, it was obvious to him: "With all these people moving in, the residential mortgage market seemed poised to take off."

Living off the sale from his window-washing business, he set to work learning the ropes of the mortgage brokering business, asking questions and calling friends and reading whatever he could get his hands on. While Jon describes himself as a self-starter, an outsider looking in who doesn't make decisions based on what it says in the textbooks, he does admit to studying the *Harvard Business Review* for case studies on what works. He studied plenty, and then in early 1994, with interest rates forecast to fall, Jon knew it was time—and he knew that with his unconventional business sense he could hit the ground running.

■ Underestimating Obstacles

The way Jon tells it, there were no problems at all. His entrepreneurial mind-set is so strong that he automatically downplays the obstacles and makes getting started as a mortgage broker sound easy. To teach himself the business, he partnered with a friend who concentrated on commercial real estate mortgage brokering. One of the basics was to get bonded for $100,000; to do this, Jon had to have $25,000 in the bank. Thanks to the money from his window-washing business, that was no problem.

The next challenge was figuring out his business plan. He wanted to keep with his philosophy of assembling an elite team of well-paid employees—if it worked for window washers, it should work for loan originators. But Jon didn't want the overhead of high salaries, so he came up with a simple solution—a commission-only compensation plan giving his loan originators a generous 50-50 split of each loan's profit. That way, brokers, who typically make $50,000 in salaries plus smaller commissions, could earn commissions in the low six figures. And instead of struggling to break into the mortgage industry, Jon hoped to attract an elite team of mortgage originators that would rocket his business to the top. To his way of thinking, this eliminated the overhead of salaries and challenged workers to give it their all. Several of his employees made north of seven figures, and a processing clerk earned over $400,000.

"In the beginning, I just said, 'I'm going to hire two or three guys a year and grow it slow the right way.'" At this point, except for the generous commission structure, his company followed the conventional mortgage broker business model, making most of its income from origination fees. Business came in mainly through the relationships his employees could forge with Realtors and builders.

Jon admits to only one difficulty: the home mortgage brokering business was a crowded field. Still he was able to make a good living. Instead of investing his profits in the stock market—which was soaring—he invested in himself and bought out his business partner in 1996.

"I don't put a lot of money in the markets," Jon says. "I invest in my own business."

Jon had learned the industry and built himself a nice little home mortgage brokerage with a good reputation with lenders. Now it was time to make some trouble for the competition. His idea was so unconventional—radio ads that called traditional mortgage firms "rackets"—that it would make people angry. But Jon didn't care: "My philosophy is it's always easier to apologize than get permission. There are things people need to hear; I will capitalize by being willing to say stuff that other people are afraid to say."

■ Building Momentum

In the mortgage world, profits lie in collecting interest. Lenders collect the interest and keep most of it, giving an origination fee to the mortgage broker. Having never worked for a mortgage company, Jon had a better idea: If I pay the closing costs instead of making the borrowers pay, borrowers will come flooding in. He got his lenders to listen because he had proven his record for originating loans in large volume—and more mortgages mean more interest for the lenders. His proposal to lenders: Give me a bigger chunk of the interest, then I'll pass the savings on to borrowers in the form of no-closing-cost mortgages, and we'll all make more money on the huge volume. In the end, the lender gets more volume and so does Jon, and everyone wins.

For example, over the 30-year life of a $300,000 mortgage, the borrower pays interest nearly equal to the size of the loan. That's a great investment for a lender. Instead of getting a small origination fee of a few hundred dollars, Jon was asking for more on the order of $9,000, out of which he would use $3,500 to pay the borrower's closing fees. "I went to these banks and said, 'You know what, I'll bring you every mortgage that I can possibly conjure up, and in return you're going to pay me thousands of dollars.'"

Jon wasn't making an idle offer; he'd already brought millions of dollars in profits to his lenders. Like a well-oiled machine, Jon's strategy worked because he gradually grew a network of people who stood to benefit from his success. Lenders, who are highly competitive with one another, knew that giving Jon a percentage of the mortgage interest would push him to score even more and bigger loans that he would bring to them exclusively.

Likewise, Jon was growing a network of loyal employees. He had an elite team of mortgage originators who would answer phones late into the night and on Saturdays, knowing that for every mortgage they brought in they received half of the fees, a staggering pay structure and far more than they would earn elsewhere. With larger fees, this elite team would have even more incentive.

Jon's other ally: radio waves. Something about the unconventional way Jon makes his pitch—unrehearsed—on a one-minute radio spot works a kind of magic. Traditional mortgage industry advertisements evoke images of a pretty house, green grass, trees in the front yard, and kids happily bouncing up and down in slow motion. Jon took the mortgage advertisement from G-rated to PG-13. He said very simply: "I have a better product and I can give it to you cheaper."

"I have a conversation in the ads just like I would with somebody across the desk," Jon says, and goes on to reenact one of his commercials: "Paying closing costs is a huge racket... You're going to spend thousands of dollars of interest over the life of your loan... Don't pay it in closing costs... It's the biggest no-brainer in the world!" These ads are like a slap in the face to mortgage brokers and the Realtors who refer clients to mortgage brokers—and an aggressive bid to poach clients from other mortgage brokers.

You can almost hear the rising blood pressure for all the Realtors and mortgage brokers when these ads hit the airwaves. Some people may say it's an abrasive ad, but it works. That's because closing costs are a huge barrier for people who want to refinance their mortgages. Offer people no fees and they'll call.

Jon even uses radio ads to recruit new employees, challenging high earners with the potential for even higher incomes. After ten years in the Atlanta market, Jon expanded into other major markets and needed to quickly add 100 mortgage originators. Instead of investing half a million dollars with a staffing agency to add the positions, Jon ran a radio ad that went like this: "If you're a top-level executive, used to making $200,000 or more, and for whatever reason corporate America doesn't want you anymore, come to my team."

It worked, and Jon says he has never had anyone quit on him. His secret? "You can't be afraid to let people make money."

The unique power of his pitch is that Jon focuses on how working with him—or buying from him—can enrich folks in ways not otherwise possible. And maybe that's the biggest no-brainer in the history of the world.

■ Taking the Next Leap

In every venture, Jon is unconventional. He doesn't even play the guitar like most people. Instead of taking lessons or consulting a book, he just picked up the guitar and played it. Over time, he's started to learn to make some interesting sounds—in his own style.

With all his unconventional success, Jon admits to one expensive mistake. He had an agreement with a bank that he wouldn't refinance clients within two years, but in his radio ads he encouraged folks to refinance their mortgages. Since there was also a clause that said the bank could choose not to enforce this at its discretion, and since he was bringing in millions of dollars as the bank's biggest broker, Jon didn't think the bank could show damages. When the bank came to him with an offer to settle out of court for around $80,000, Jon countered with zero dollars. "Next thing you know, I got hit for $563,000," Jon recalls. "They played my radio ads in court and that was the end of that. That's a hard lesson learned: cutting my nose off to spite my face."

Part of the unconventional approach is rolling with the punches, and when Jon retells the story about the lawsuit, he shows what he's made of. Financially, it was a wash because his aggressive refinancing ads had brought him enough business to pay the penalty. And it was a valuable lesson.

Regardless, Jon is doing well. In 11 years, he's built a company valued at $100 million and is still coming up with ideas. His latest is a Web-based software application that he designed to revolutionize the mortgage business even further.

His advice to you and me is that we not only listen to his unconventional ideas but also come up with our own: "I never looked at the billionaires and thought those guys were any smarter than I was. They're regular guys who came up with something and were not afraid to act on it. You'd be surprised how many ordinary people come up with phenomenal ideas but just don't ever do anything about it."

Try this: The next time you go somewhere new and confusing, like an airport, don't ask for directions. Just sit back and get a feel for the lay of the land, the flow of foot traffic, and the way the terminal is laid out. If you approach it as a game, it will soon be obvious to you where your gate is. Or try this: pick up a new instrument, like Jon picked up the guitar, and start playing around with it with no lessons or instructions. Just use the instrument, and gradually you will start to make your own music.

And in your work as you approach each task, remember Jon's secret: "Listen to what you're thinking—just because it hasn't been done before doesn't mean it's not a good idea!"

Chapter Nine

Steve Bercu, CEO and Owner of **BookPeople**

Keep It Weird

Steve Bercu isn't just a successful small business owner, he's an inspiration to bored, successful 50-somethings everywhere to find a second career that keeps them young and earns a good living. His story is a weird and wonderful testament to what one person can do when he or she decides to make a change.

It started when Steve was tired of everything being the same. He needed to do something different. So Steve retired early from his law practice and built a business around being weird: a huge independent bookstore that combines the individualistic spirit of Texas with the tastes of a highly educated, artsy community. His store, BookPeople, boasts a staff of outgoing salespeople, which is practically unheard of today at most large bookstores. Besides books, the store also sells such quirky gifts as Sigmund Freud action figures, fake mustaches, and "Keep Austin Weird" T-shirts. The unusual strategy hit a nerve. "Keep Austin Weird" became a rallying cry for his independent bookstore and small businesses all over the city. Steve's weird movement spread beyond Texas, and his slogan continues to pop up on bumper stickers around the nation. In his office,

Steve shows off a photograph of a Humvee outside Baghdad, complete with a "Keep Austin Weird" sticker.

Steve's store, BookPeople, is a huge independent bookstore, the biggest in the country. Despite stiff competition from several big-box book retailers in the area, BookPeople has a steady 3 percent sales growth. And in 2005, it was awarded the book world's highest honor of bookseller of the year. Steve scoffs at the conventional wisdom that independent bookstores are a dying breed. For skeptics, he quotes this figure: only 8 percent of books are sold online. What booksellers need to focus on is giving customers a different experience that they can't get anywhere else. Something a little weird.

Steve started out as a very un-weird law student. He was never all that enthusiastic about practicing law; it just seemed like a good way to earn a living. When he graduated law school in the 1970s, he went into business for a while selling the forerunner of today's fax machine. When that fizzled, Steve went to work for legal aid, earning a small salary representing people who couldn't afford a lawyer.

Eventually, Steve went to work in law in El Paso with a partner and made good money doing criminal defense and personal injury cases. In 1976, when Texas liquor laws changed, he and his business partner bought a piece of land in El Paso and opened the city's first bar, the New Buffalo. It was fun and exhausting. Even though staff did most of the day-to-day work, Steve spent a lot of time at the bar overseeing and enjoying. After four years, they got a good offer on the land and sold it.

In 1980, he and his law partner moved to Austin, where Steve worked on more high-profile cases and built some wealth. The experience of owning the bar and seeing the land appreciate in value got him thinking about real estate, so he bought and sold land and houses and invested in the stock market. Then middle age happened.

As Steve approached his 50s, he wanted a change from the courtroom's endless repetition. "The facts were different in each case, but the format was the same," Steve recalls. So in 1991, he up and moved to Mexico with his wife and their two-year-old daughter. Steve still kept his hand in the law and flew back to the states occasionally for cases, but mostly he relaxed and proudly watched his daughter become bilingual.

That's when Steve came across something weird. It was a bookstore named BookPeople, owned by Philip Sansone. Steve met Philip at a party on one of his trips back to Austin. The bookstore owner said he wanted to expand his bookstore into a huge new location, but he needed money for building and inventory. It was unusual, but Steve figured he'd invest in it.

When his daughter reached school age, Steve moved back to Austin.

■ Starting from Scratch

After its expansion, BookPeople didn't do so well. Steve walked in as CEO of BookPeople in 1999 when he and his coinvestors mutually agreed that he should close down BookPeople's business affairs. The place was in sad shape, and with his legal expertise, he thought at least the value of the land, building, and inventory could keep it from being a total loss. Instead, Steve fell in love with the place.

BookPeople was a proud symbol in Austin, where the store had grown out of tiny Grok Books in the student slum district at the edge of the University of Texas. The first time the store moved, in 1985, it added general interest books to its Eastern philosophy collection and blossomed into a roomy 7,500-square-foot store. When Steve invested in 1994, BookPeople moved to its current huge 40,000-square-foot location. At the time, it had 300,000 titles. It went from Austin's biggest bookstore to the country's biggest bookstore.

But that last expansion coincided with some big bookstore chains moving into the Austin market, and BookPeople was losing money in a big way. Since Austin has the number one book-buying community in the country, per capita, Steve figured BookPeople should be doing great, despite competition from the new chain superstores and the Internet. After taking over as CEO, Steve started working the floor to see what was up. He found the real problems: no inventory controls and bad customer service.

Steve grew up learning about retail at his grandmother's Dallas toy store. At age ten, she gave him the model airplane department and told him he would run it—even ordering and tracking stock. "It was a cool thing," Steve remembers. He ran it pretty well, making a few mistakes along the way, such as when he enthusiastically ordered 100 small motors for the model airplanes and barely sold a handful. That's when he found out how important it was to research products before ordering—and not to overorder. By the time he was in high school, Steve fully understood the retail business and how to keep up on trends to figure out what customers wanted.

It was obvious to Steve that he knew how to make BookPeople profitable. He rolled up his sleeves and geared up to save his store.

■ Underestimating Obstacles

"You need to change." That was Steve's prescription for his employees. "A lot of people in small bookstores spend a lot of time whining about all the new competition," he told them. "So there are six Barnes & Noble stores and two Borders Books in the area. Who cares? We're not competing for identical people; we're competing for *our* customers. You've got to keep up with the times."

Steve outlined his plan to the staff. They had to work at making the place stand out from the competition. He couldn't do it with atmosphere—BookPeople's huge store wasn't cozy and funky like most independent bookstores. But he could do it with the service. BookPeople needed to have a remarkable staff of outgoing, friendly salespeople who had no problem approaching strangers and striking up conversations about books.

Steve made it clear to the 95 employees that they could stay if they were willing to change. "I didn't get rid of everyone on the low levels; I started at the top," he says. He fired the old marketing director and hired a new one who could put on great book-signing events, and he fired the floor supervisor who wasn't very good at motivating staff and found one who was great with people. "People got the message right away that the boss was serious," Steve recalls. If they wanted to stay, the other employees needed to get on board with the new model of selling. No more sneering at customers, even if they ordered so-called lowbrow books. If a customer wanted a book and it wasn't in stock, employees needed to do everything they could—even call the local Borders to find it. Steve was serious about beating the competition with customer service. Within 18 months, there was a huge turnover; about 80 percent of the employees were new hires.

Steve uses an essay test to screen prospective employees for their knowledge of books. In interviews, he talks to people about the kinds of books they like to read. But more important, he looks for natural-born salespeople. "I'd rather hire someone with the personality to sell and then teach him or her about books," he says. "You can learn books, but you can't change your personality."

Another change was to cut down on BookPeople's massive inventory. Steve cleared out one whole floor of book inventory. In the mid-1990s, before the Internet took over, it made sense to stock a lot of inventory. No longer. Now that he could order books from his suppliers with just a click, there was no need for all those extra books. Steve leased the extra space as office space to Whole Foods, which was headquartered next door.

Just as he was hitting the ground running, a good thing happened—but at the time it seemed like the worst thing. Steve got wind that Borders was planning a new store across the street from BookPeople.

■ Building Momentum

"I didn't want to whine; that's un-American." Steve says. "Competition is good." On the other hand, he found out in 2001 that the city of Austin was giving an incentive package to lure Borders and other chains into the development. "It's an unfair competitive advantage to give tax dollars to another business," Steve says. He joined forces with a neighborhood CD store, Waterloo Records, which also stood to lose if Borders moved in, and formed Austin Independent Business Alliance, a chapter of the American Independent Business Alliance.

Like any well-run retailer, BookPeople and Waterloo had a huge e-mail list of customers. Using those lists, in July 2002 the two stores sent e-mails asking their customers to write to the city council expressing opposition to the incentive package, which was up for a renewal vote. Within ten days, Steve started getting calls from city council members saying they'd gotten *thousands* of e-mails in opposition.

Meanwhile, BookPeople flourished. "We got so much publicity," Steve says. BookPeople's efforts to stop the tax incentive appeared on the front page of the local newspaper sections about once a week for at least a year. A local weekly alternative paper did a feature about them. "There was huge public interest in the issue," Steve says. "Essentially, without Borders signing up to come across the street, we would have had an incredibly more difficult time pulling off the turnaround."

That's when Steve's weird campaign began. He'd heard the countercultural slogan "Keep Austin Weird" over the years, but now he gave it new meaning. Steve and the Waterloo Records owner put their store logos on a bumper sticker that read "Keep Austin Weird, Support Independent Business." They split the printing costs for 5,000 bumper stickers and gave them away for free at their cash registers. They ran out in ten days.

Meanwhile, a community group, Liveable City, joined with BookPeople and Waterloo to commission an economist to do an economic impact analysis on what would happen to local businesses if the city's proposed development went forward. By fall 2002, the study came up with a staggering statistic: spending money in a locally owned business adds 3.5 times the economic impact as spending the same dollars in a chain store.

"It all comes down to labor costs," Steve says. The chain business model cuts down on administrative costs by having much of the behind-the-scenes work handled at company headquarters. So independent companies end up spending a lot more on business services, like accounting and legal services. It's not bad; it's just a fact of business. CivicCommunities, the economist's firm that did the study in Austin, is repeating similar economic studies all over the country.

Now, Steve is a minor celebrity in Austin. And his bumper stickers are all the rage. He and the CD store gave away 145,000 "Keep Austin Weird" bumper stickers in two and a half years. The first time Steve saw one of the bumper stickers on a car, he got excited. Now he sees them all over the country, and other communities are borrowing the phrase. Plus, the independent business association he helped start now has 350 members. "It's been a lot of fun," Steve says.

Incidentally, Borders withdrew from its lease in 2003. It said it had nothing to do with the controversy, just generally slow economic conditions.

■ Taking the Next Leap

In 2005, Steve gave a speech to the 100 or so graduates of the Bookseller School run by the American Booksellers Association at the Book Expo of America in New York City. His advice: "There are massive segments of the market available for bookstores in small resort communities that are too small for the chains." Think small, quaint book shops, he advises, with a little weirdness and character. For instance, the Reading Reptile children's bookstore in Kansas City, Missouri, is decorated to look like a busy family's living room; and The Tattered Cover in Cherry Creek, Colorado, looks like an old-time bookshop with spiral staircases and leather armchairs. The whole point, Steve says, is to give customers a retail experience they can't find anywhere else.

Instead of whining about Internet bookselling, which accounts for a fraction of the market, Steve tells booksellers to pay close attention to what it feels like for the customer entering your store. "You're selling the customer experience," he says. "People can buy everything online; they don't have to leave their bedrooms anymore. But 92 percent of the time people choose to go to a store to buy books. They want an experience."

Steve also advises all business owners to know their local politicians: the mayor, city council members, and county legislators. Volunteer to serve on some boards or commissions and make yourself known, he says. You never know when there will be changes that affect your business, whether it's tax law, street closures, or incentives for competitors.

For now, Steve is just enjoying the success at BookPeople. At age 62, he feels young and invigorated, plus he's making a good income. And he's still active in the independent business association he helped start, which has grown from 2 members to 350 businesses and remains a strong voice in Austin.

Getting into a second career as you reach retirement age might seem a little weird, but Steve recommends it. "It's a really good thing to challenge yourself instead of resting in front of your TV," he says, "or resting at the business you've been doing for 35 years." Instead of resting, Steve advises, you should "keep it weird."

Chapter Ten

David York, Founder of **Barking Hound Village**

Resiliency

Picture this: seersucker pants, red shirt, blue blazer, a tie with stars and stripes, and white patent leather shoes. Then picture this same guy selling fireworks in a rainstorm, selling apple dumpling franchises, and running a five-star pet hotel. It sounds like the makings of a great screenplay to me—the story of a colorful, caring, and utterly resilient man.

To say David York has overcome a few setbacks is an understatement. A tornado swallowed his teenage fireworks stand; he barely scraped his way through college; he went to his first real job interview looking like a clown; and his family outvoted him and forced the shutting down of his first franchise. After all of that, he has consistently bounced back and ended up a wildly successful entrepreneur in the exploding pet care industry.

David, 45, is now the owner of Barking Hound Village, a doggie day care and hotel that he started in Atlanta and has grown to seven locations in Atlanta, Austin, and Dallas. His start-ups, setbacks, and successes are inspiring—and hilarious. "There's a lot of walls you have to climb over," David says of his starts in business. I'll say. He's the epitome of underestimating your obstacles.

Growing up in Sikeston, Missouri, David already showed resiliency at age 14 when he set up his own fireworks booth near the highway in front of his farm. It was two weeks before Independence Day, and he'd built the fireworks stand with help from one of his family's farmworkers. The first day of business was incredible, until a tornado disintegrated his fireworks shipment that afternoon. David remembers his mother advised him to quit, but he just went and ordered more fireworks. After all, he figured he'd gotten his bad luck out of the way early. Sure enough, in the following two weeks he made $5,000. He did this each June for three years, and then he went to town and bought himself a new Cutlass with his savings at age 16.

After college, David wasn't sure what to do. His dream of being an architect didn't pan out, mainly because he couldn't hack calculus. So David worked at a bank and then a local department store. But he dreamed of bigger things and subscribed to the *New York Times.* That's where he saw a Macy's ad for management trainees. On a whim, he sent in a résumé. To his surprise, Macy's called him in for an interview.

When he arrived in New York, David had the kind of crisis that would have made most people cancel the interview—the airline lost his luggage. With no time to shop for a new suit, he set out for the interview dressed as he was on the plane in a casual blue-and-white-striped sports jacket. On the way, he had a quirky impulse—he bought a red tie with a star pattern and put it on. He looked like a flag.

"I thought, I might as well dress wild because they're going to laugh at me anyway," David recalls. Sure enough, as he sat in the waiting room, people were coming out of their offices to sneak looks at him. When they finally called him in, the interviewer said he'd heard people talking about the guy dressed like a flag but figured they were joking. Everyone had a good laugh; David was a good sport.

After a second interview, he was hired into the management training program. They gave him this feedback: "If you've got the nerve to come to an interview looking like that, then you've got what it takes to work at Macy's." David moved up through the ranks—with the nickname "the stars 'n' stripes guy"—all the way up to buyer and private label developer. He might have made a life-long career at Macy's if it weren't for his mom's apple dumplings.

By the early 1990s, cinnamon roll shops like Cinnabon were popping up everywhere. Whenever he went home, he would bring back some of his mother's frozen apple dumplings and serve them to friends in New York. People went crazy for them. It got to the point where they would call him when they knew he was going to Missouri and ask him to bring them a batch of his mom's frozen dumplings. On one of these trips, David and his sisters hatched a plan to open a little local bakery, Dumplin's, and serve baked goods. Soon they had a little 600-square-foot shop in Sikeston that was bringing in great profits.

■ Starting from Scratch

To get things started, David and his sisters each put in $10,000 to set up the first Dumplin's store. They made back their investment in the first three months. Labor was cheap in Sikeston, and so was rent. Plus, everyone knew their family, and the food was great. Soon his sisters had expanded to a larger space across the street and added a lunch menu.

In the first few months of Dumplin's, David's sisters ran the bakery and he came home every few weekends to help and advise. Very soon, he started getting calls from entrepreneurs who wanted to buy a franchise license to open their own Dumplin's store. David was amazed. He hadn't intended to sell franchises, yet people who had been through Sikeston and enjoyed some of the amazing apple dumplings wanted to start their own Dumplin's.

David had no intention of working in the restaurant business or of moving back to Missouri, but that's what ended up happening. Some local Sikeston lawyers directed him to a St. Louis law firm that specialized in franchises. David didn't know anything about them, so he just made an appointment, listened to the lawyers' advice, and did what they told him. Eventually, he quit Macy's—even though he was making good money there—because the chance of making more as a franchiser was too good to pass up.

Since Cinnabon franchises were going for $25,000 apiece plus 3 percent annual royalties, David picked that number out of the air and put that price on his Dumplin's franchises. "It just got rolling," David recalls. He had franchise buyers already lined up as they'd been calling him for months. In the first five years, he licensed and helped open 30 restaurants in nine Southern states. "People would eat there and would love it," David says. The stores practically sold themselves; home-baked goods as a concept were very *in* at the time, and the stores were mostly opening in smaller markets where labor and rent were cheap.

David likes to say that it was totally luck, but he put a lot of work into the franchise. First of all, he had to learn a lot. He didn't know what a convection oven was, had never seen a three-compartment sink, and didn't know how to make egg salad or bake bread. "I just figured things out," he says. When he first moved back to Missouri, he bought a new car and within five years had put 290,000 miles on it from driving around doing training, scouting out real state, and meeting contractors. His sisters mainly took care of the Sikeston store. It seemed like the franchise business was a sure thing.

■ Underestimating Obstacles

No entrepreneur lives in a vacuum. There are always disasters and influences that you don't foresee, just like David's fireworks stand being destroyed by a tornado. This time, the disaster was family strife.

Evidently, starting a franchise requires a lot of capital to build a strong organization. It's pretty common for newcomers to the franchise business to make the mistake of spreading themselves too thin and not spending money on growing the corporate structure enough to support the stores. David fell into this trap as well. "I was up against a wall," he says. They needed an influx of cash, and David was prepared to go look for investors, but his sisters didn't want any part of it.

Meanwhile, David was working round the clock to open more franchises. His sisters saw only the financial risk of continued expansion and wanted to sit still and just operate the Sikeston store. They wanted no part of the huge franchise empire that David envisioned. While he couldn't convince his sisters, David was still getting calls from franchise buyers and more Cinnabon restaurants were popping up everywhere.

"It was a terrible thing for my family, and we didn't speak for a few years after it," David says. "It was a bad situation." He was frustrated, knowing the franchise's potential and how big it could be, and his sisters said they just didn't want to do it. They didn't understand the concept of getting investments and were afraid of the risk.

On the other hand, David had taken a pay cut when he left Macy's in order to build the franchise into something big. He hadn't taken much of a salary for himself out of Dumplin's because he wanted to put all the money back into growth. There seemed to be so much demand; the Sikeston store made money like crazy; and people wanted to buy more franchises. David was convinced they could remedy their cash flow problems and build it up. To this day, he still says he could have done that. But his sisters owned two-thirds of the company and David owned only one-third. Their husbands backed them up and insisted that David stop expansion plans. They bought him out, although since there wasn't much cash on hand, it didn't amount to a fortune.

Meanwhile, David nearly put himself in the hospital from physical exhaustion. After he got out of Dumplin's, he was ready for a rest and something new.

■ Building Momentum

When one door closes, another one opens. After the fiasco with his family, an exhausted David landed in Atlanta because it just seemed like a good place for a new start and he'd heard real estate values were going up. He figured he'd buy a fixer-upper house, remodel it, and take a vacation on the profits. But after the first house, David saw he'd found a great opportunity. Two, in fact.

It was 1996, just before the Olympics were held in Atlanta, and real estate was skyrocketing—especially in the Ansley Park neighborhood where David had bought his house. Most of the people in the neighborhood were elderly, and as they saw prices going up they wanted to cash out of their homes without dealing with Realtors and without fixing up and showing their homes. They started calling him and asking if he'd like to buy their houses.

David had a little money to invest and great credit, plus he'd met a doctor with money to invest. The two became business partners and started buying and rehabbing houses. These were the times of the dot-com bubble, so there were plenty of people walking around with money to buy houses. And the Ansley Park neighborhood was one of the up-and-coming addresses in the city. Real estate prices were going up tens of thousands of dollars overnight. For example, he bought a home for $525,000 and sold it seven days later for $750,000 without even touching it. "It was unbelievable the money we were making," David recalls. All in all, he and his business partner bought and sold 18 homes in two years.

How did David know how to renovate homes? He didn't. Just as with the bakery, he saw an opportunity and rode the wave. And still another enterprising opportunity came his way.

After making a small fortune in real estate, David figured he'd earned the time for some relaxation and travel but couldn't find a good place to leave his dog. He tried a pet sitter for Sophie, his springer spaniel mix, but the sitter left the dog for two days without food, exercise, or time to go out. The dog and the house were a mess. Asking around with neighbors, he found out there weren't a lot of options. That's how Barking Hound Village was born.

David had stumbled onto another trend. The pet industry has nearly doubled in the past ten years, with Americans estimated to spend $35.9 billion on their pets in 2005. The pet industry is now the seventh largest retail segment in the country, according to the American Pet Products Manufacturers Association. Those figures put the pet industry at 60 percent larger than the U.S. toy industry.

David didn't need statistics to tell him that in 2000, when the first Barking Hound Village opened in one of the properties he had bought in a retail area. Featuring doggie day care as well as boarding and a bakery with dog treats, it was an instant success. David drew on what he'd learned from his past mistakes. For one thing, he had a business partner who was interested in growth—the same doctor who had invested in some of his real estate deals. And when it came to day-to-day operations, David hired enough staff so he wouldn't end up in the hospital with exhaustion.

David seized new opportunities as they came up. For example, some customers had problems with big rowdy dogs that couldn't be left home alone all day and needed a lot of exercise. So David opened the Barking Hound Village Athletic Club, a place to leave dogs while their owners were at work so they could play with other dogs as well as their human caretakers. Barking Hound Village even started to offer dog birthday parties (really), a deli with chicken rice pies and poochie pizzas, and a luxury spa.

Barking Hound Village was expanding like crazy. When David's business partner took a radiology post in Austin, they opened a Barking Hound Village location there.

From the beginning, Barking Hound sponsored an Atlanta pet rescue group, which now places 30 to 40 dogs a week that otherwise would be euthanized. He says he does it because it helps keep his enthusiasm for coming to work each day and not for the public relations. But the PR sure helps.

In 2003, David met Hope. It happened one day when a friend from Texas faxed him an article about a dog that had been shot and buried in a field. But she wasn't dead. A neighbor found the dog crawling down the road, rescued it, and took it to a vet. David immediately called the vet, who had named the dog Hope, to check on her and donate money toward her vet bills. After a few months, the vet called back and said she needed a good home and maybe more surgery down the line. David flew to Texas, drove back with Hope, and nursed her back to health. Now she lives with one of his employees.

Although he didn't do it for the publicity, he ended up with a flood of media. Local news, CNN, newspapers, and even a Japanese magazine. Everyone was caught up in the story of Hope and her recovery at Barking Hound Village. David had done it again.

■ Taking the Next Leap

What did David want to be when he grew up? An architect. And when that couldn't happen, he just kept looking. Tons of people have amazing home recipes, tons of people notice real estate values going up in their city, and lots of people noticed there was a need for quality pet care and boarding. However, most people do nothing about these seemingly everyday opportunities. David York always did. His advice: "Just pull out the stops and dream."

"My biggest strength is I'm never smart enough to see the downside of anything," as David sums up his incredible success in business. Everything has its drawbacks, he says, but David trusts himself to figure things out and make them work. His motto: "Roll with the hard knocks."

That's what sets David apart. He's always ready to harness what he has, underestimate the obstacles, and take another first step. Sure, he made a lot of mistakes in the restaurant business, but he also learned from those mistakes.

Although he regularly works 60-hour weeks, David says he's not as hands-on involved with taking care of the operations. But he does like playing with the dogs. As he tells this story, he's interrupted a few times by dog owners and dogs coming in to say hello. That's what keeps him going, he says. Like any 24-hour-a-day service business, Barking Hound Village can be stressful. David says it's like an all-night coffee shop—it never closes. And during the busy holiday season, if Atlanta is hit by a freak snowstorm and employees can't make it in to work, David is there taking care of the dogs. But most of the time he has time to focus on growth and plan expansions. In 2005, he opened a Barking Hound Village in Dallas.

Early in life, David didn't let a tornado put him out of the fireworks business. Again and again over the years he showed that same resiliency. Even in college, when his grades were barely enough to graduate, he stayed upbeat. If he couldn't wow Macy's with his college transcript, he would wow them with his upbeat attitude and outrageous clothes.

Back in his late 20s, David left his safe management job at Macy's to take his chances as an entrepreneur. Now, nearly 20 years later, he's glad he did. Fences were mended with his family, and he's not bitter about the problems with Dumplin's.

Those earlier problems didn't kill him; they made him stronger and more resilient.

Chapter Eleven

Alan Thompson, Founder of the **Off The Grill** franchise

Work the System

Tired of his sales job in commercial real estate, Alan Thompson built his own restaurant system by making a lot of mistakes along the way. Now his system has him at the top of a growing, multi-million-dollar empire—the Off The Grill restaurant franchise. Alan's story shows the restaurant franchising business from both sides: franchisee and franchisor.

Alan's career took a winding route, but he always had a system. Whether it was cutting lawns, selling real estate, or selling take-out dinners, Alan broke down his business ideas step-by-step and figured out how he was going to make money. For example, as a kid, just like me, he started cutting lawns for people at $5 per yard. But then he realized he could get other kids to do the work for $2.50— that's a 50 percent profit margin if you don't count the gasoline. Soon he had a lawn-cutting empire. By age 15 he had bought his own car with $1,500 cash. That's a lot of green for a kid.

Alan's lawn-cutting work took him to some surprising places. Cutting grass one day at an office building near his college, Alan met a businessman looking to buy the property. They got to talking, and the older man shared his system for selling real estate. Alan was hooked. Originally, his plan was to get a pharmacy degree and partner with a family friend looking to expand his drugstore business. But Alan couldn't hack his organic chemistry class, and real estate started to look very good. His father was an engineer, the first in his family to ever go to college, so there was a lot of pressure for Alan to finish college. He didn't, and instead started working for sales commissions in commercial real estate.

The thing about commercial real estate is that it's feast or famine, and at first Alan saw only the feast. He got on board in 1984 at the beginning of the savings and loan crisis, when banks were heating up the market by unloading foreclosed commercial properties. Alan hooked up with an attorney and former banker who needed a salesperson to work their simple system. They would fix up the foreclosed properties for the savings and loans, lease them up, and sell to investors—all at a profit to the savings and loan and to themselves. "We made a lot of money doing it," recalls Alan, who went from making $5 an hour to $20,000 a month. "At age 21, you don't see an end to that. I was young and stupid and I thought making a living was pretty easy. I thought I was invincible."

Business is all about change, and the market opportunity that made for easy money in commercial real estate eventually changed. It happened when the federal government's Resolution Trust Corp. stepped in and changed the game by selling off the savings and loan properties before they could be renovated or leased.

As one developer after another went belly up, Alan saw the writing on the wall and started hunting for the next opportunity. "I needed a cash register," Alan says. In other words, he needed a business that brought in a constant flow of money because his commercial real estate sales job was running into some cash dry spells. A trip home to Huntsville showed him the way.

Visiting his girlfriend back in his hometown, the couple wanted to order out for dinner but had a taste for something besides pizza. His girlfriend had a flyer from Steak-Out, a new take-out restaurant, so they gave it a try. "The food was incredible," Alan recalls. It was so good that by the end of the week he'd called the franchise founder; a few months later, Alan bought the rights to his own Steak-Out.

As it turned out, the restaurant franchise business was simple. It just wasn't easy.

■ Starting from Scratch

Alan's family jumped on board. His younger brother had some cash to invest, and between them the brothers put in $150,000 to build the 2,000-square-foot restaurant. His older brother, fresh out of the Army, and his wife were the operators; his mother kept the books; and his father helped with the design and layout of the store. Alan would do the marketing and advertising.

From the time it started in 1991, Alan's first Steak-Out location did well, running at a 25 percent profit margin—which is great for the restaurant industry. Steak-Out offered a simple chicken and steaks menu for delivery or take-out. For that first year, Alan still held on to his real estate career, selling properties in several states through a toll-free phone number from his office at the back of the Steak-Out restaurant. As the real estate business waned and the restaurant took off, Alan flowed with the changes. He decided to put all his effort into being a Steak-Out franchisee.

Working as a franchisee can be hard for entrepreneurs to get involved in because franchises impose limits and restraints on a business model. A certain percentage of sales must be paid every week to the franchisor; another fee goes toward national advertising; and the restaurant has to serve food according to exact specifications— right down to the grade of meat. For people escaping corporate life, that kind of structure might rub them the wrong way. A franchisee needs to have a mix of entrepreneurial spirit and the ability to follow rules and regulations. That can be a tough mix.

The idea behind franchises is that they run on a proven business model based on the mistakes that other people have made. A great franchise model can be a very secure business. But Alan had signed on with a young franchise that hadn't made many mistakes yet and had a bit of growing to do. As Alan expanded, opening up more Steak-Out locations throughout Tennessee, he and his family improved the systems and passed this on to franchise headquarters.

Alan became president of the franchise association, where franchisees share best practices and support each other. He was the biggest Steak-Out franchisee with five restaurants to his credit. Alan had not only learned the system, he also had improved the system.

All was well until 1995, when the franchise founder sold the business to a new owner.

■ Underestimating Obstacles

In hindsight, Alan knows exactly where he went wrong with Steak-Out: "I was smart enough to get advice but not smart enough to take it."

His main problem with the new owner boiled down to ethical concerns over price controls. The new owner was forcing franchisees to buy meat from a supplier who didn't always have the best prices or highest quality. Alan wanted to persuade the new owner to change, but the more he lobbied, the more he met with resistance. The disparity between franchisee and franchisor was headed toward a legal battle. So he found a former copy store franchisor mogul who had been sued by his franchisees and asked his opinion. The advice: Avoid litigation at all costs and just sell the five franchise restaurants. Alan wouldn't consider it.

"I'm right and he's wrong," Alan insisted, and set out to sue the new franchise owner.

The problem with litigation, Alan found, is that usually the person with the deepest pockets wins. Alan didn't have the deepest pockets. Even though he had five restaurants, he really couldn't afford the kinds of legal bills that began to rack up. Eventually, as the lawsuit dragged on, Alan had to give it up. He went through a Chapter 11 bankruptcy, mainly because it enabled him to get out of his Steak-Out contracts. After dropping the Steak-Out name, he turned around and sold the restaurants and property for a cool $1.2 million.

What was he going to do now? Make the leap from franchisee to franchisor. To do this, Alan took his profits from selling his five restaurants (after expenses it was only about $500,000) and plowed it into opening his own restaurant. While he says now that he probably needed an amount closer to $2.5 million to launch a national franchise, he didn't know that then.

"At a young age you don't take risk into consideration," Alan says.

Alan called his new restaurant Off The Grill. The menu was upscale: steaks, chicken, salmon, pork chops, grilled vegetables, and salads. And the restaurants combined delivery and take-out with a "fast casual" dining area. Since Alan was bound by a noncompete agreement in Nashville with Steak-Out for two years, he set up his first Off The Grill restaurants in Phoenix, where a couple of friends agreed to help him open two restaurants. Those first two restaurants did well. When people asked if they could franchise, Alan was off and running. He would invite the prospective franchisees to the restaurant, where he would show them the ropes. If they signed a franchise agreement, he would fly to their city a few times, walking them through the process of finding and building a restaurant.

That's where Alan's commercial real estate background came in handy. After getting a few site listings from a commercial Realtor, Alan would do his own research. First, he looked for good visibility from the road, easy exit and entry, and easy access for delivery trucks. Then he got demographic figures, such as income levels and number of households living within three miles of the location. He got his figures from Esri Business Solutions, one of many firms that offer business locator demographics.

Alan didn't advertise his Off The Grill franchise to potential buyers, but at least once a week a customer would come in and ask how to start an Off The Grill. Many were out-of-towners in Phoenix on vacation. By 2001, he had sold 20 Off The Grill franchises around the country.

Alan did his best to support the franchisees. For instance, when franchisees complained about overwhelmed grill kitchens during the dinner rush, Alan gathered some of his key employees at his Tennessee lake house and brainstormed about the issue. They came up with the innovation of two separate grill lines: one for take-out and delivery orders and the other for the dining room.

Little did Alan know there was another problem looming on the horizon that would blindside him and the entire nation: the terrorist attacks of September 11.

In this vulnerable position, Alan was hard hit by the tight economy. Borrowing money to build more restaurants became impossible for a while. By then, Alan's noncompete agreement had expired, and he had moved back to Nashville to start up Off The Grill restaurants. He was spread out all over the country, from Raleigh, North Carolina, all the way to San Diego, California. "When my franchisees started hurting—and stopped paying royalties—I was too spread out to support them the way I needed to."

It costs a lot to enforce contracts. When franchisees quit paying royalties, Alan tried to marshal goodwill instead of trying to force the stores to pay royalties. After a while, it was obvious that the struggling operators didn't have the money to pay. In July 2004, Alan was in bankruptcy court again.

That bankruptcy was the turning point, Alan says. That's because he had some great assets to sell: the Off The Grill brand name, his upscale meat delivery business model, and 20 restaurants with franchise agreements. He caught the attention of some big-time franchise operators, a group of investors who owned a portfolio of over 100 restaurants. They had the cash to grow the brand and allowed Alan the opportunity to continue to run the company. "It was the best thing I ever did," Alan says.

◾ Building Momentum

Alan found the missing piece to his franchise system: market saturation. It's the lifeblood of the franchise game because it cuts costs to manageable size. For instance, a radio ad might cost $5,000 in a big city. If only one store is footing the bill, it cuts profit margins too deeply. If 20 stores share the bill, that's only $250 per store. The same goes for all kinds of expenses, from food delivery to cleaning services.

It's a chicken-and-egg problem. "In the beginning, you have to sell to mom-and-pops or you'll die, but mom-and-pops will also kill you because they don't have expertise or money to invest," Alan says. To succeed, a franchisor needs big-time operators with deep enough pockets to build dozens of stores in one area, but in order to get their attention he or she first needs the small operators.

Finally, Alan had the backing of big-time operators, MRCO LLC, with a whole portfolio of Taco Bell, KFC, and Pizza Hut restaurants.

The first step was to concentrate on one area: the Tennessee-based operators chose the Southeast. Now, there are 20 Off The Grill franchises, and every new store that opens helps leverage the success of the other stores. About 60 to 70 percent of Alan's restaurants succeed. He's hoping to get the figure up much higher in the coming year.

Now that he has market saturation in a few cities, Alan can be picky about the kinds of operators he sells franchises to. For example, many operators think they can save money by using one grill line for both dine-in and delivery, even though the Off The Grill system calls for always using two grill lines. The problem comes when the line can't handle the volume: customers get slow service and never return. On the other hand, good operators are the ones who really care about customer service. "It's hard to pinpoint these guys," Alan says, because everyone who wants to buy a franchise license says they'll be the best owner you've got."

With MRCO LLC involved, the snowball has started to roll. Alan has more time to improve systems because the new owners brought a network of other investors. MRCO LLC is one of the top 100 franchise operators in the country, and its interest in Off The Grill gets the attention of other big operators looking to build dozens of restaurants.

Getting investors was a turning point. For one thing, the additional support staff freed him up to get the bugs out of his system. And that's the point of a mature franchise: the mistakes have been made and fixed. In a mature franchise, operators don't have to reinvent systems; they simply have to follow the rules. Alan thinks Off The Grill has finally reached that point.

Now that it's easier for Alan to spread the word about his franchise concept, it's also easier for him to improve the system. For example, this year food costs dropped 3½ percent because Alan had time to concentrate on negotiating deals with food vendors. He's also been improving the layout of the restaurants to handle more customers as the concept catches on. The best part: As all these improvements continue, Alan attracts even more interest from franchise operators.

He can also be picky about where new stores open. For instance, if someone calls him from California wanting to buy the rights to a restaurant or two, he tells the caller it's going to be a few years before Off The Grill reaches the West Coast again. When he was younger and struggling to sell franchises, Alan wouldn't turn anyone down—even if that wasn't the wisest way to go.

■ Taking the Next Leap

Ever notice how business and love relationships are a lot alike? In a relationship, what you really love about someone also ends up being what you hate about them. In business, what makes you successful is also the same thing that can kill you. With Alan, he says his persistence is good, "but persistence is also what kills me." If he hadn't been persistent, he might have quit and Off The Grill wouldn't exist; but if he'd been less persistent, he also might not have taken the financial hits that landed him in bankruptcy. "You have to know when to fold 'em," Alan says.

For example, when he was a Steak-Out franchisee and had differences with the new owner, he now says he should have sold right away. And when he overextended Off The Grill and financing dried up, he wishes he had looked into selling before things got as bad as they did.

Luckily, there are second chances and things are working just fine for Alan. With his investors and a proven system, he's making his dream of owning a franchise empire come true.

Alan advises anyone who wants to start their own franchise to have a good estimate of how much money will be needed. For instance, it takes at least eight stores to get a decent market share in an average-sized city. So at the very least, you need to concentrate on getting eight units in one area—either open them up yourself or find partners who can open some.

Another part of the system is the cost-to-sales ratio. For example, it costs $350,000 to open an Off The Grill store, and average sales per store are $800,000 annually. Even with royalty and ad fees of 6 percent of sales, that's a good cost-to-sales ratio. On paper, a store could be profitable in one year. Even as he explains that, Alan laughs and says the problem is that an operator can't start planning on being profitable the first year because, as he knows, unexpected things come up.

Also, anyone who wants to start their own franchise should know about "barriers to entry," or the things that make a concept hard to copy. As a fast-casual dine-in and delivery restaurant, Off The Grill is hard to copy because it takes special packaging and cooking techniques to keep food hot and appetizing all the way to the customer's front door. But a sandwich shop doesn't have many barriers to entry because almost anyone can copy it.

In the future, meal take-out and delivery will be even bigger, and Alan thinks Off The Grill is in a position to take a huge share of that market. He's got a point; there aren't many restaurants in the country that deliver grilled steak dinners. And he thinks his restaurants can handle the demand. In Nashville, Alan's family still owns an Off The Grill that does $1.5 million in sales per year. That's lot of volume from a little 2,200-square-foot unit. He thinks the store could handle up to $2.5 million in sales because it's designed to handle volume.

The future looks good for Alan. With Americans eating at home more but cooking less, the take-out and delivery food market is growing fast. Alan's expertise is to make a streamlined system to turn out dozens of well-run restaurants.

Now, Alan's system is working for him.

3

Notice Your Network

Just as a bow and arrow leverages a hunter's strength, noticing your network leverages your relationships with people around you. The H (harness what you have) and U (underestimate your obstacles) parts of the HUNT are internal steps; with N (notice your network) you're moving outside yourself to find people who possess the information, skills, and resources that complement yours. This step can be exhilarating because it makes you notice your surroundings, the people around you, and their talents.

Twenty-first-century hunters rarely work alone. In the HUNT for business success, we all have a network of allies, partners, friends, and even perfect strangers who we can call on to help us reach our goals. These helpers can assist in bringing our vision to reality—if we would only notice and ask for help. Successful ventures may come from one person's vision, but one person's vision is never accomplished without help. In the entrepreneurial mind-set, there is a method to noticing your network.

First, always take advantage of the low-hanging fruit: the obvious stuff that's right in front of your face waiting to be harvested—like a professional conference, an entrepreneurship class at a nearby college, or your brother-in-law the attorney. Go to the obvious places to find help to launch your idea. And when you go to these obvious places, be a good hunter and don't make a lot of noise—do a lot of listening.

Second, there are the other hunters you know or meet along the way. Although they are your competitors, they may also be your allies. After all, it takes a team of hunters with specialized skills to take down a bear. The clever man sets up the trap to catch the bear; the fast man runs ahead to scout out the bear; and the strong man finishes the job after it's caught in the trap. It's the same thing in the business world. You've got your clever sales engineer who describes a product, the fast-talking person who gets you in the door for the meeting, and the skilled salesperson who negotiates and closes the deal. And with a big deal, there's plenty for everyone.

This brings us to the third part of noticing your network: reciprocity. Helping other people is the best way to get them to help you. You can get anything you want in life if you help other people get what they want out of life. That means spreading around the wealth when you are successful.

Noticing your network is more important than it ever was before. As our economy continues to evolve, we rely more and more on specialization. Even computer programmers specialize. Any successful business is built with many talented people working within their strengths and united by a vision. There's so much power in that.

Noticing your network compliments—and complements—the strengths of others. Who wouldn't feel flattered and complimented by someone who asks for their advice? When you ask someone for advice, you let them know that you respect and trust them. That's a huge compliment. You also let that person know that you have skills that complement theirs. When you ask for advice, you may be hooking up with someone who will hunt with you. For example, when computer programmers Dave Babson and Ken Romley asked for business advice from a consultant, the consultant ended up so impressed with how their skills complemented his that he went into business with them.

Noticing your network is also about power. You empower people when you ask them for advice, because you invite them to be your teachers—and teachers always say that they learn best when they instruct others. In return, noticing your network empowers you as well.

Noticing your network leverages your strength—and the strengths of others—to catapult your vision into reality. While everyone in this book noticed their network, the people in the next five chapters had secrets that really got them noticing their networks:

- **The power of PR.** Matt Lindner relates to everyone, and he understands the importance of public relations. He uses his outgoing nature to network with everyone he meets—his customers, his suppliers, local magazines, and his employees—to spread the word about his bar. He gives away freebies to customers, treats employees well, and uses outrageous, attention-getting advertising that has the public and local media loving him.

- **Charm.** We live and die by our customers. Chuck and Roberta Slemaker charm their bed-and-breakfast guests and do a huge repeat business. They also charm their competitors (and even state lawmakers) to come around to doing things their way. The Slemakers know that the secret of charm is figuring out what other people want. Focus on how you can fulfill the other person's desires and that person will find you charming.

- **The power of friendship.** Dave Babson and his friends Ken Romley and Michael Doernberg have an amazing synergy. Alone they are each pretty talented; together they are a force. Pooling their skills, they came up with valuable software solutions for large corporations and were able to cash out for millions—three times over.

- **Mentors.** Starting young in business, Susan Flores wanted to start her own coffee shop in an exotic location, but she didn't know where or how. It was her mentor who guided her with his experience, wisdom, and encouragement she needed to open her first business.
- **Communication.** From the time he was on the high school debate team, Tim O'Leary knew the value of good communication. All his life, he could present and sell an idea. He leveraged the skills of a television production studio and became an infomercial guru who sings the praises of mass marketing.

There's so much power in your network. Notice it. Leverage it. In business, when someone talks about leverage, we figure they're talking about borrowing money. In a very basic sense, leverage *is* about borrowing money; but leverage is also about borrowing talent and power. When you leverage your network of friends, family, and acquaintances, you leverage their talents and power to bring your vision to reality. In return, your network also benefits from your success.

If you're not leveraging your network, learn the secrets of people who are.

■ Chapter Twelve

Matt Lindner, Founder of **Cans** ■

The Power of PR

PR = Public Relations. PR is one of the most powerful forces in the modern universe and essential to the success of the next story.

Wouldn't it be great to own a bar? After earning a management degree in college, Matt Lindner got fed up counting glasses each night at the corporate-run restaurant he managed for $500 a week. Instead of living the corporate nightmare, Matt, 33, is now living every man's fantasy of owning his own bar.

This is my favorite story in the book because most men reading this—including me—have had the fantasy of owning a bar or night-club. (Undoubtedly, a few women have, too.) We have this vision of sitting at the back of the bar with a few of our best friends, gazing over the crowd and thinking, This is *my* place. On any given night, the more beer we drink, the closer the dream gets. We get it from the movies, from watching Ray Liotta and Joe Pesci in *Goodfellas* sitting in the back of the Tree House, surrounded by their friends. Not only do they own the bar but they also own the town. There's a certain power and mystique in the bar business. Remember Steve Rubell of Studio 54 fame, virtually running New York City as he held the keys to the hottest commodity in the greatest city on earth. Steve

Rubell even had the audacity to turn away Cher at the door. I would have paid to see that.

Matt says that it's pretty simple to understand why we have this fantasy—beer, women, and cash—and I'm not going to argue with him. But he'll also tell you success in the bar business is about properly harnessing the power of public relations. Right from the start, when he was sleeping in his first bar because he couldn't afford an apartment, Matt put his customers first. Sometimes he says he feels like a teacher in a junior high school. But no matter what kind of ruckus his patrons cause, Matt and his partners carefully manage their public persona, making sure they are in control and happy to be part of the fun.

"Whether we're happy or not, we're in the public eye, and we can't be grumpy and bitter," says Matt, who calls himself a service industry freak. Matt's obsession with relating to the public is like a pebble tossed in a pond, sending out ripples in an ever-widening circle. He figures if he treats people right, they'll come back and bring their friends—and where there are friends, there are *hot* girls (another small secret to success he confesses to). Also, if he treats employees right, they'll pass that on to his customers.

And when it comes to noticing his network, Matt can teach us all a few things. Look at his public relations efforts: He partnered with a high school buddy who used to work in liquor promotions; he makes customers into regulars by handing out freebies (everything from key chains to coveted Chicago Cubs tickets); and he endears himself to the media with his outrageous, attention-getting ads ("Thank God for CANS!" which pictures a large-chested woman holding two cans of beer). Pure genius.

Besides being great at networking, Matt has another secret for starting from scratch: he knows that life is way too short to put off his dreams. As a teenager, he almost had all his dreams smashed in a horrific car accident. Rescuers had to use the Jaws of Life to pull him from the tangled mess. Amazingly, he survived with only a few busted teeth and a messed-up knee. After that close call, he resolved to enjoy life to the fullest and pursue his dreams at all cost.

Maybe that's why when he found himself working under someone's thumb at his first job after college, Matt didn't put up with it for long. His first job out of school was managing a restaurant with a lot of responsibility but not a lot of control. The place was profitable and run with corporate cost controls—which made sense. But what didn't make sense to Matt was the way he felt unappreciated and underpaid. Sound familiar? If it does, this is a story about doing something about it and harnessing the media along the way. One day, after counting glasses, he just up and quit and went back home to Chicago. He arrived in the Windy City with a burning desire to build a place he could call his own.

■ Starting from Scratch

When Matt showed up at his parent's home and told them he was going to open up a bar, they thought he was crazy. But they never said don't do it. Instead, they asked if he knew what he was doing. His answer: "I think so."

Matt, who was 24 at the time, asked around with some business brokers and found a struggling bar that the owners were anxious to get rid of. To raise money, he sold his car and borrowed $5,000 each from five college buddies; the bar's owners financed the rest, and he agreed to pay them back at $800 a month for the next four years. His story is the perfect example of how, if you want it bad enough, you can always find the money to make it happen. Let me repeat: You can always find the money to make it happen.

Since Matt's nickname is Bird, he named his first bar The Bird's Nest, and for a while it really was his home. In those early months when Matt and a college buddy ran the place, they slept in the bar because they couldn't afford an apartment. For showers, they went to the health club down the block. After they could afford to hire bartenders and staff, they would take turns crashing at the apartments of their staff.

Their days were filled with taking care of the hundreds of details. The Bird's Nest needed work: the tables needed cleaning, the floor needed sanding, the walls needed painting, the bar needed to be refinished, and chipped glasses needed to be replaced. The to-do list was a mile long. Matt and his friend worked 20-hour days and still didn't get it all done before the grand opening. The work wasn't difficult, but it was overwhelming. In the afternoons, when the bar opened and customers arrived, Matt put his cares aside and put on a smile.

Unlike the hundreds of guys that come up to Matt and talk about how much they want to open a bar, Matt knew how to HUNT. He harnessed his college marketing degree, his experience working in restaurants in college, and his likable personality with what he was really good at and loved to do. Then he worked like crazy.

On Sundays, Matt and his first business partner would sleep into the afternoon until the first customers came knocking on the back door to wake them up. In return for helping clean the place, Matt would give them free beer. He wasn't getting rich, but he made enough to pay back everyone who loaned him money. And he was having the time of his life. The thing about Matt is he didn't mind hard work and getting very little sleep as long as he was building something of his own. That's true for most people starting from scratch. After six months, Matt started to see results. He could finally hire a manager, find an apartment of his own, and stop sleeping on the floor.

After a few years, Matt wanted to grow the business. Instead of a neighborhood bar like The Bird's Nest, he envisioned a chain of bars with multiple locations. To do that, he partnered with his high school friend Jay Runnfeldt (who had worked in liquor promotions) and a college pal, Tommy Wang. In 2003, the threesome opened up Cans Bar and Canteen, a bar themed on serving beer from "retro" aluminum beer cans, and music and movies from the 1980s and 1990s—decades during which the target clientele were coming of age. Cans now has locations in Chicago and Milwaukee, with more planned. The trio also owns two other bars, Salud (an upscale tequila lounge) and Four (a hip nightclub).

With his success at The Bird's Nest, which he sold to his long-time manager, Matt was able to find a network of investors for Cans. By now he's an expert at hunting for opportunities.

"There are a million creative ways to figure out how to open up a place if you really want to," Matt says. Since most guys have this yearning to open their own bar, he says it's pretty easy to get someone to buy into the dream by loaning you money. The key is to find the right circle of investors who have cash and would like to say, "I'm one of the owners."

■ Underestimating Obstacles

But it wasn't all easy. There was the time Matt was low on cash and bounced a check—five ways—and the time a rowdy drunk threw a cement block through his window. Matt can laugh at it now, but when hard times hit, it isn't nearly as funny.

Back when he was first starting, cash was tight, and Matt tried to stay one step ahead of the bank. It didn't always work. Not having money can be downright embarrassing, especially if you own your own business. Once when he was sharing an apartment with a girlfriend, he wrote a check to her for his share of the rent. His business account had been running low, but he wrote himself a paycheck thinking it would skim by. That check bounced, so his check to his girlfriend bounced, then her check to the landlord bounced, and everything just bounced along. Matt felt like a loser, and when he went to the bank to explain, he got a lecture on how he owned the company and should have known there wasn't enough money in the account.

Other times, Matt used his personal credit card to buy liquor for the bar and just hoped that when his charge bill came later that month he would have made the money to pay for it. He did, but back in the early days he was always walking a very fine line.

Then there was the time that Matt broke his own rule and lost his cool with a customer. It had to do with little candle lamps that sat on each of the tables at The Bird's Nest. They cost about $20 apiece, and every night one or two of them turned up missing. With all the money issues Matt was dealing with, the thievery finally got to him. Here he was, an honest businessperson who made it his business to show respect for his customers and staff, and petty thefts were costing him hundreds of dollars a month.

One night, someone saw a lamp under a guy's jacket, so Matt ended up angrily accusing the customer and kicking him out for trying to steal the lamp. Even though he'd lost 50 of these little lamps, this one was the straw that broke the camel's back. The next morning, Matt returned to the bar to find a cinder block thrown through his window with a nasty note attached. Right then, Matt saw that the cost of letting the customer get to him had taken a $20 loss and turned it into $500 of window damage. For the greater good of the business, Matt learned to put aside his personal feeling and to "let it go, and go with the flow." That's hardly the attitude we see in *Goodfellas*, but it's the reality of any service business.

Even now, with the business running successfully, the hours can be long. For example, after taking his fiancée out to dinner for her birthday this year, Matt had to return to Cans to oversee a promotional event.

Still, guys come up to Matt every Saturday night, when one of his bars is open till four AM, and say, "Man, you've got it made!" He agrees, but he also tells them, "You know I'm going to bed at 5 AM, but I have to get up at 8 AM and go back to work." Like anything else, Cans is a real business. People just see the glamour of it and think that selling beer is all laughs and profits, but a successful bar isn't a hobby and has to be run like a tight ship with standard inventory control and cost controls. When we go to a bar and witness someone like Matt, we just see the glamorous side and want to be part of it.

For all the work, Matt is glad to own Cans. He loves coming to work in the hip part of Chicago, not wearing a suit unless he wants to, and being in the business of having fun. And on some nights, maybe he does feel like he's living out a scene from *Goodfellas*.

■ Building Momentum

In the bar business, Matt and his partners understand that customers are really part of their network. If someone spends a lot of time at the bar or comes back a few nights in a row, Matt always has a few Cubs tickets around to hand out as a personal thank you. And he's always giving away key chains, T-shirts, and hats. Because if people feel good about their time at Cans, they'll come back and bring their friends.

And Matt likes to impress his customers. Last year he was one of the first Chicago bars to outfit waitresses with Palm Pilots so they could send orders to the kitchen and bar without walking back. Imagine how impressed you'd be to have your waitress take your order and chat with your table and then have your drinks and food delivered before she even has a chance to get to the kitchen. And the gadgets keep the kitchen from getting slammed with a bunch of orders all at once. It's just another way Matt gives Cans customers a reason to feel pampered and special.

Cans also cultivates a reputation for having a good ratio of women to men. Matt says he does that by keeping the place clean and having bathroom attendants, even though the place is mainly just a beer joint. He also makes sure women are treated politely and feel safe—that includes nicely dressed bouncers checking IDs at the door instead of scary, leering goons. Women want to feel safe and be able to dance and relax—so that's the atmosphere Matt gives them.

And then there are the Cans ads. Maybe they're not the most politically correct ads—in-your-face would be a better way to describe them. But they get a lot of attention. They're the kind of ads that guys rip out of magazines and pin up on bulletin boards. You get the idea. The billboard and magazine ads feature a play on the word *cans,* tag lines that push innuendo and shocking photos. Of course a few people call in and complain, but mostly the ads are tongue in cheek and folks appreciate the humor. Matt and his partners enjoy sitting down and brainstorming the ads, and they have a graphic designer who comes up with the photos. In Chicago's advertising circles, those ads generate some fun buzz about Cans. It's just another way that Matt gets people talking about his bar.

He's even got himself pegged as an expert on the subject of beer cans. The *Wall Street Journal* quoted him in an article about the increase in canned beer consumption. When you know the power of PR, word gets around.

Another way word gets around is through employees, and Matt tries to keep good feelings there too. If the bar gets slammed, he and his partners will get their hands dirty and pitch in busing tables, washing dishes, and mopping floors. Even now, when they own four bars, the partners will still pitch in, and employees know they can ask for help. That translates into employees who have respect for themselves and do their best, Matt says. "They'll do things because they know we would do them too."

■ Taking the Next Leap

Even though Matt and his partners took their first steps already, they're constantly taking next steps. In 2004, they opened Cans Milwaukee, and later in 2005, Cans Charlotte. When people come up to him and tell him he's lucky to be doing so well, Matt thinks, We're not even close; we've got loftier goals now. The partners have other people caught up in their plans as well: Matt's cousin, who worked as a consultant for Deloitte & Touche, left a prestigious job and came to work on their expansion.

What's the draw? A bar, or any business, is the direct reflection of its owners. Matt loves to walk around incognito at Cans and listen to what people are saying. Little do they know the owner is standing nearby listening to them talk about what a great time they're having and how much they like the Palm Pilot service or the music that's playing. Ninety-five times out of 100, the comments are positive. When they're not, if someone is complaining to friends about the music or the bartender is dissing them, Matt takes care of things in that calm way he has.

Matt's advice to anyone looking to start their own business: Do it. It doesn't have to be a bar or nightclub—although he makes it look so fun—it could be some other idea you've got floating around in your head. So much of business is marketing, Matt says, so if you have an idea, find someone who knows about that industry and brainstorm about marketing and development.

Even Matt's parents, who thought he was crazy to open his own bar, are now his biggest supporters. They've invested a little into his ventures too. After they got over the shock, Matt says, they would come to his bar and be happy to see the crowds. Now if they're downtown for dinner, they stop in at Cans or any of Matt's other clubs and bring their friends. Even though they were worried he would lose his shirt, his parents are proud. Matt's father talks about Matt more than he talks about himself.

Sure, a start-up takes time, money, and energy. But working for a paycheck takes a lot out of you too. Matt remembers how tired he would feel at the end of the night working as a restaurant manager. It wasn't the industry; it was being under someone else's thumb that was tiring him out. After ten years as his own boss in the bar and restaurant industry, Matt has built up an asset and a reputation as an owner who comes up with catchy brands and outrageous advertising. He's not living large. Instead, he's putting money where it belongs: advertising, growth, repaying investors, and paying valued employees well. And at night, when he sits at the table with his two best friends, they look out over the happy crowds and think: this is ours. What would you give to have that?

In the future, Matt's not sure what will happen. If he and his partners build Cans up to a nationwide chain, they might sell and cash out. Or maybe not. Whatever happens, Matt will get there using his own wits and his knack for networking and PR.

Through hard work and the power of PR, Matt really is living the dream.

■ Chapter Thirteen

Roberta and Chuck Slemaker, Founders of the **Alpenhorn Inn B&B**

Howard and Lynda Lerner, Former Owners of **Red Crags B&B** and
Founders of **Inn Caring**

Charm

Lots of couples dream about going off and starting their own bed-and-breakfast (B&B) in some charming tourist town. This is a story about two couples who actually lived that dream. They also fled forest fires, were raided by the feds, found unusual items in guests' rooms, and made friends with people from all over the world. Their stories show the exhilarating reality of B&B ownership.

Roberta and Chuck Slemaker loved to entertain, but they hardly had time for it because work was taking over their lives. Now, instead of long hours on the road and the threat of layoffs, they run the Alpenhorn Inn B&B in Big Bear, California, where their days include leisurely dining, golfing, and skiing in a charming mountain retreat.

Howard and Lynda Lerner have a more earthshaking story. Literally. After the 1994 Northridge earthquake forced them out of their California home and into the streets to wait out the aftershocks, the couple looked at the devastation and hysteria surrounding them and decided to leave town. To rebuild their lives, they bought a bed-and-breakfast in Colorado Springs.

The two couples' stories have a lot in common. Both had business skills that they'd learned in corporate America; both wanted to escape stress; and both took the all-business approach to run their inns with cash flow projections and lots of research. And they both know how to charm their guests.

But the two stories are different as well, and they show the two main approaches to starting a bed-and-breakfast. On the one hand, you can start your own inn from the ground up and customize it to fit your plans—that's what Robbie and Chuck did. On the other hand, you can buy an existing B&B and adapt to it—as did Lynda and Howard. Either way, a B&B can be a great escape—for the guests as well as the owners.

In 1995, Californians Robbie and Chuck realized they needed to get away from stress. The hardworking couple realized they'd dug themselves into a hole with work, but neither one wanted to admit how miserable they'd become. For Robbie, her job as human resources manager became excruciating when her employer started downsizing. "All I did was help managers lay off people," says Robbie, who stayed up nights worrying that her own job might be next. And Chuck's project manager consultant job meant he pretty much lived on the road 70 percent of the time. One day, they put it all on the table and decided to do something about it. Since they loved entertaining—and didn't mind hard work—the idea for a bed-and-breakfast came up right away.

Howard and Lynda were also looking to get away from stress and into semiretirement. They had stayed at bed-and-breakfasts and always fantasized about starting one of their own, and now that they needed to move to a new home anyway, the time just seemed right. With Lynda's skill running a middle school classroom (and later working in a personnel office) and Howard's financial skills as a CPA, they figured they could take it on.

■ Starting from Scratch

The gold standard in the bed-and-breakfast industry is the "diamond" rating system developed by the American Automobile Association. Most B&Bs have three diamonds, which means they maintain a high level of service and are usually run by a husband-and-wife couple with very little staff. On the high end are the four-diamond inns, which have 24-hour staffs to answer phones and take care of guests.

Robbie and Chuck wanted to go the luxury route—mainly because they wanted to live in a luxurious atmosphere. They'd discovered the Big Bear Mountain area in Southern California on vacation, but in the mid-1990s, there were no bed-and-breakfasts there. Now, you can look at that statistic in two ways: no B&Bs mean no competition, but it could also mean that the remote area couldn't support a B&B. Chuck says he figured it was worth the gamble.

But Chuck was also methodical and careful. To forecast business volume, he went to the Professional Association of Innkeepers International (PAII) to collect industry data on business volume for the average B&B in the western United States. Armed with that information, Chuck and Robbie went house hunting.

One thing about Chuck and Robbie: they love to schmooze. Even while house hunting, they were talking to Realtors and getting an education about California property values. In the mid-1990s, houses were going for about $100 per square foot in the remote areas of Southern California, where many of the houses were seasonal vacation homes. The common wisdom at the time was that these prices were soon going to skyrocket. Even if their B&B flopped, the property would be a great investment.

By December 1995, Robbie and Chuck bought three pieces of property with bank mortgages: a five-year-old 2,600-square-foot house for $260,000, a vacant lot and 500-square-foot cottage for $50,000, and a 1,000-square-foot house for $100,000. All three properties were bought with bank mortgages and renovated with a $500,000 construction loan. They kept their day jobs and worked at

planning and renovating for nearly three years before the Alpenhorn Inn would open for business.

Howard and Lynda took a different approach. Their idea for a
bed-and-breakfast was more of a whim. One day, tired of hearing
Howard complain about his job, Lynda cut out an ad from the *Los
Angeles Times* for a B&B for sale. The couple traveled to Colorado to
look at it and right away fell in love with the Red Crags B&B. They
envisioned cooking elaborate breakfasts, charming the guests, and
coming up with marketing plans. Using savings and some money
from an inheritance, Howard and Lynda bought Red Crags.

Even though Howard and Lynda made their decision on a
whim, they were also driven to succeed: if they were going to run a
B&B, it was going to be a successful one. The first mistake most
B&B owners make, Lynda says, is to run it like a hobby. From day
one, she and Howard wanted to run it like a business. Before they
opened their B&B, they attended a B&B conference and learned everything they could. It turned out that many B&Bs run at about
40 percent occupancy, some even lower than that. The couple decided to do everything they could to boost cash flow and have a
higher occupancy rate.

One way they planned to get more cash was to add two rooms
to the six-room inn. That meant investing $125,000 to remodel the
adjacent carriage house. Right away they figured that would
change the financial picture. When they bought it, the inn had only
35 percent occupancy and six rooms. Howard and Lynda calculated
they could bring it up to at least 50 percent occupancy right away,
even with the two extra rooms.

The couple also decided to try a new kind of advertising: a Web
site. It was 1995 and most folks didn't really know what a Web site
was. But at the B&B conference, Howard and Lynda met a man promoting Web sites who developed their site for only $300. The first
week they launched the site it paid for itself with a $1,000 reserva-
tion. "I was giggling," Lynda says. "Nobody did it then; we outmar-
keted everyone."

■ Underestimating Obstacles

Howard and Lynda were able to open their doors to paying guests just one month after they purchased Red Crags—that's the advantage of buying a going concern. The only change they made to the business was to market it more aggressively and expand by renovating a carriage house into two extra rooms. They called their approach "pure business," because they were set on improving cash flow and making profits.

After attending a B&B conference, they plunged right into the B&B world. The first time a toilet backed up, Howard grabbed a plunger and unclogged it while Lynda headed off guests and directed them to the other bathroom. Early on, they learned to smile even in the middle of a mess. They had their share of rough spots—unreasonable guests, unexpected repairs, and long hours—but the whole time they kept telling themselves this was better than the rat race in California. Their saving grace was that they always kept a repair fund ready and hired help whenever they needed a break. That first year was a crash course in the hospitality industry, but they were turning a profit by the end of their first year.

In contrast, it took three long years—and a $500,000 construction loan—for Robbie and Chuck to transform a 2,600-square-foot home into the 6,400-square-foot Alpenhorn Inn. Cities like Big Bear can be backward when it comes to their antiquated codes, but the small-town mentality was also a plus—officials were willing to work with them to make their vision come true. For example, Big Bear's city code defines a B&B as five rooms or less, so Robbie and Chuck's B&B was classified as a hotel—which would have required building a loading dock in the back. Why a loading dock? Because city officials thought that a hotel would need room for big trucks bringing in shipments of food. All Chuck had to do was explain that the last thing they needed was a loading dock in the back. Instead, he told them that Robbie just makes a few trips to the store each week, and if it made them feel better, she could bring the "shipments" in through the back door—quite a compromise—and the city let them continue operation as a B&B.

The renovation years—from 1996 to 1999—were hectic. Chuck was still consulting and Robbie was still working as a human resources executive at an aerospace firm. She worked until April 1999, when they moved from their home in Palo Verde up to Big Bear. Chuck's last consulting gig was December 2000.

Besides financing, the biggest thing to get used to for people who have never been in the hospitality industry is the day-to-day nuttiness of the B&B life. Howard and Lynda were a little shocked by their guests at first. Like the time a maid discovered a handgun under the bed. Howard, who is terrified by the word *gun*, was beside himself and immediately called the police. Then there was the time the kitchen ceiling directly underneath a guest's room was visibly shaking as Howard and Lynda served breakfast. The couple giggled along with the rest of the guests when the man and his wife came down to breakfast with a story about his jumping rope for his morning fitness routine.

For Robbie and Chuck, their most unusual crisis was in their first year when Alpenhorn was raided by the state's alcohol and beverage control board. Three armed agents actually swooped down on their B&B one Saturday to inspect the place. It turned out that even though they had a liquor license, they weren't allowed to serve certain beverages, such as after-dinner liqueurs. Flabbergasted, they took the citation and paid the fine. Who reported them? Another B&B owner who had moved into the area—sounds like fierce competition in quiet Big Bear!

Can you imagine someone practically storming your front door for breaking a law you didn't know existed? That might be enough to discourage a lot of business owners. But Robbie and Chuck faced this obstacle head-on. It turned out there was no license that would allow them to serve liqueurs, so Chuck contacted the California Lodging Industry Association (CLIA), met with lobbyists, and made a $500 campaign contribution to a state senator. A year later, the governor signed into law a new kind of liquor license that allowed California B&Bs to serve any alcoholic beverage known to man as long as it was included in their room rates. To this day, the couple is jokingly known in the CLIA as the "bandit B&B owners." What a great example of how to deal with obstacles: humor, charm, and finesse. The couple even set out to gain the friendship of the B&B owner who had turned them in!

But all the charm in the world couldn't overcome a raging forest fire. That was Robbie and Chuck's other big struggle. It happened in late 2003, when wildfires were ravaging Southern California after a five-year drought. Big Bear, located right in the middle of a national park, has only three access roads; and one of them was cut off by fire.

One Sunday morning, they were serving guests breakfast and heard that the forestry service had issued a voluntary evacuation. Incoming traffic had already been cut off, and people were only allowed down the mountain, not up. Chuck was being his usual charming self, joking with the guests over breakfast, when he mentioned that maybe the inn guests were now classed as refugees. That got a good laugh until an hour later when the forestry service issued a mandatory evacuation. "We hustled the guests out of there," Chuck recalls, "and Robbie and I hustled around trying to figure out what to do." Robbie grabbed their dogs, Chuck took the computer, and they bundled into the car and headed away from the mountain. As they ran out the door, Chuck changed the message on the answering machine to say they were closed as a result of a mandatory evacuation order and didn't know when they would reopen.

The evacuation cost them a lot of business; luckily, it didn't cost them their inn. Two weeks later, when the fires were under control, Chuck and Robbie reopened. While the fire had stopped ten miles from the inn, many people wrote off the Big Bear area as a vacation destination. People called to cancel their reservations, not wanting to travel just to see burnt trees. Chuck and Robbie spent a lot of time getting word out that their part of the woods was unscathed.

As their stories show, the B&B business turned out to be a great decision for both couples.

■ Building Momentum

It takes a special kind of person to be in the bed-and-breakfast business. Even with forest fires, quirky guests, and alcohol raids, there are always phones to answer and toilets to clean. But both these couples say the real secret to their businesses is being able to charm their guests.

Think of it: people go to B&Bs because it's like being a guest in someone's home instead of a sterile hotel. B&B guests want to talk to the owner, strike up a relationship, and, hopefully, return again soon. Recently, Chuck analyzed his business statistics and found the biggest growth wasn't from the Internet or advertising—Alpenhorn's biggest growing segment was return business. Howard and Lynda don't have exact statistics, but they know they have a huge return customer base; to this day, they still maintain friendships with some of their European guests.

Now, charm isn't something everyone is born with. But it's something that can be learned. After all, charm is about engaging other people and figuring out what they want. Focus on the comfort of the person you're talking to—and do whatever you can to give them what they want—and that person will find you charming. Some people want flattery, some people want to be amused by your stories, and some people just want great service and a polite attitude. Caring about what your customers want is great for any business. Charm pays off.

And then there's the Internet. Nothing can get the word out about you and your business to more people—faster—than the Internet. For B&Bs, the Internet has revolutionized the old start-up plan of opening the door, relying on word of mouth to limp along on one or two guests the first month, and then three or four the next, if you're lucky. It doesn't work that way anymore. A brand-new B&B opening its doors for the first day now has as much opportunity as the place that's been in business for ten years. The reverse is also true. "If you're not on the Net, you're gone," Lynda says.

That's because with so many products and services available online, every business owner is competing with a Web site. And you know the old saying, "If you can't beat 'em, join 'em." Internet advertising even made Robbie and Chuck open their doors before they were really ready. They had posted photographs of the house under construction, as they renovated from a one-bedroom home to an eight-room inn. Immediately, they started getting e-mail inquiries and phone calls, even though some of the rooms weren't finished. "One day, things were moving so fast, we just announced that we're open," Robbie recalls.

A Web site isn't going to automatically make you rich, but it sure can jump-start a new business. Yet technology goes only so far. The other piece of the puzzle is to back up Internet advertising with human beings. Robbie and Chuck go to the extreme: they have a human being available to answer the telephone 24 hours a day.

Answering the phones round the clock isn't a necessity in the B&B business, as Lynda and Howard can tell you. They ran a more laid-back inn, with an answering machine for backup when they weren't available. Technology—Web sites and answering machines—will never take the place of the staff and owner.

■ Taking the Next Leap

In the six years since Chuck and Robbie opened their B&B, they say the best thing they did was invest in great property. The asking price of the three pieces of property was $410,000, financed by mortgages. Ten years later, the property is worth $2 million, which they found out when they consolidated the three mortgages into one loan. The care they took in finding their location paid off. They now have nearly two acres that are centrally located east of the Big Bear village and only a half mile from the summit and five blocks from a lake. "To put together two acres in the heart of town was nothing short of fabulous," Chuck says.

Someday, if the property values escalate to $3 million, Chuck and Robbie figure they will sell and enjoy a prosperous retirement. Chuck sees himself growing bonsai trees; Robbie would put more time into her hobby of attending dog shows. For now, they like living in a luxurious resortlike community and working about as hard as they did in their corporate jobs. Only now, they have an asset worth millions. And they can take off midweek for a game of golf or a few hours of skiing. Not bad for a couple who didn't have time to even sit down together for dinner.

This year, they hired a publicist for $500 a month to try to get the word out about Alpenhorn and the Big Bear area to more tourists. They're sharing the publicist with another B&B. Interestingly, those other B&B owners are the very people who reported them when they first opened. Now that's the power of charm.

As retirement age approached for Howard, 63, and Lynda, 59, the next step in the B&B business was to sell Red Crags in 2004. The couple has come up with a new business that they call Inn Caring. They "babysit" B&Bs for other operators who are taking time off for vacations or to recover from illnesses. They also teach classes on how to be an interim innkeeper. With the money they made on the sale of Red Crag (which they sold to the same person they bought it from), they're living in comfortable semiretirement in Colorado Springs and plan their innkeeping schedule around extended visits with their daughter and grandchild. As Lynda says, running a successful B&B and then selling it earned them "the freedom to be grandparents."

That's the kind of freedom that their jobs wouldn't have given them. Now, instead of working in their jobs in the Los Angeles rat race—with a few weeks vacation per year—the couple has control of their lives and schedule.

Thanks to their hard work and charm, both of these B&B owners are living a labor of love and looking forward to a comfortable retirement—or maybe they're already there.

Chapter Fourteen

Dave Babson, Cofounder of **Burl Software** and **Marathon Group**

The Power of Friendship

In the world of business, one plus one should equal three, and two plus one should equal five. Such is the story of a dynamic trio of business partners who formed a leading software company based in the Raleigh, North Carolina, Research Triangle Park. Yearning to make his mark on the world, Dave Babson left his corporate dream job to start a company that only he and his friends understood.

"We jumped without a place to land," Dave says, without a hint of regret. A sort of ringleader for the group, Dave likes to brag about how young and foolish they were. And how determined they were to succeed. Fourteen years and millions of dollars later, Dave jokes about taking that first leap into the unknown at age 24. All they had were ideas and the ability to write software. Above all, they were friends first, business partners second.

Using their ideas and friendship and just plain living by their wits—these three guys made millions of dollars by not following plans. Instead, they followed opportunities. Their flagship product, Revolve, for example, started out as a tool to make blueprints of old mainframe programs. In the mid-1990s, it quickly morphed into the world's leading Y2K tool, generating over $100 million annually.

Thinking fast, following opportunities, and being flexible turned out to be more important than planning.

For Dave, leaving his corporate job at Bellcore—his dream job—was a hard decision. In his first two years on the job, Dave had already racked up four software patents, a $5,000 bonus, and his picture on Bellcore's annual report. In the end, it was that $5,000 bonus (for a $60 million project) that pushed him into taking the leap to being an entrepreneur. Dave figured if he could build software worth hundreds of millions of dollars, he should be making a lot more money.

■ Starting from Scratch

When Dave and Ken Romley started Burl Software in 1991, major corporations were being forced to upgrade from mainframes due to the burgeoning PC industry. This meant plenty of opportunities for computer engineers who could design systems to do that, but there was also a lot of risk. Those were tough economic times, and Dave and Ken both knew unemployed computer engineers who were resorting to yard work just to earn some money. Talent and education were no guarantee of success.

Ken saw how corporations were struggling to move information from mainframes to PCs. In his job at Price Waterhouse, Ken saw firsthand that companies had no idea how to harness the power of the new PCs. The business advice of the day called for caution and slow, measured steps. As a junior employee at Price Waterhouse, Ken's ideas for how to integrate PCs with mainframes were pushed aside. He was too young, just out of graduate school, and he was basically told to shut up and listen. After that happened a few times, he took his ideas and jumped ship.

When Ken approached Dave with his ideas for how to move information out of mainframes and into PCs—a task that every corporation in the world was facing—Dave saw the huge opportunity. He left his job at Bellcore and the two went shopping for office space.

With no money, unfinished software, and no clients, they needed something cheap. They found a place offering a shared conference room and receptionists to answer the phones, but they couldn't afford the first space they were offered. "Can you show us something without windows?" Dave asked. Still too expensive. "How about something smaller?" Finally, after they couldn't even afford the smallest office, they pressed for something cheaper. Half joking, the rental agent showed them a storage closet for $300 a month. They took it.

Even though the closet didn't give them windows or space, it gave them something more important: credibility. So what if they were crammed into a closet? At least they had a professional-looking address for their business cards, an answering service, and a conference room to meet guests. Within weeks, they had written software to move data from mainframes to PCs. With new business cards in hand and experimental software, they went looking for a place to test it.

In the software industry, a product is never finished until it's beta tested in real-world conditions at real companies. People won't take software seriously until it's been beta tested by a prestigious company. In North Carolina, RJR Nabisco was one of the most prestigious. But two young guys peddling some untested software would never get through the front door at RJR Nabisco. Not without contacts.

That's where Mike Doernberg comes in. Dave and Ken met him when they went looking for help from Ernst & Young's entrepreneur consulting group. The consultants weren't impressed with the young software coders' vague business plan and threw their business cards in the trash after they left the room. But the presentation wasn't wasted. Mike heard their presentation and was impressed by their passion for inventing software. He literally picked their business cards out of the trash and called them on his own.

At Ernst & Young, Mike had personal contacts with big names in corporate America. He knew their wifes' names, their kids' soccer teams scores, and their favorite brands of beer. Thanks to Mike's personal contacts, Dave and Ken ended up making a presentation in the offices of RJR Nabisco. But they almost screwed it up. Mike warned them that the number one thing they should absolutely *not* do was get off the script. "These guys are nervous about buggy software," Mike said, so don't push the experimental software to do anything that might "lock up" the program in an unending loop. Of course, in their excitement, Dave and Ken got off the script attempting an impromptu command that froze the system.

From across the room, Dave saw the screen lock up. Dave and Ken's eyes met for a panicked second. The RJR people hadn't noticed yet, but within seconds everyone would see that the program wasn't responding. As the onscreen icon continued to spin, Dave thought fast. He got up, walked across the room, and pretended to trip on the power cord—cleverly unplugging the computer. Once the computer rebooted, they got back on script. The presentation was saved. And RJR beta tested the product—with good results.

When they tell the story now, you can hear the incredible dynamic that these guys have. Together, they feel invincible.

■ Underestimating Obstacles

Dave likes to say that obstacles are just directions for what you have to do next. Burl's first obstacle—once they beta tested their product—was that they still had no money. They couldn't even afford the fee to set up a table at a trade show. To their way of thinking, that meant they should go to a trade show anyway. So they loaded a computer into a car and drove to a trade show in nearby Virginia.

Sitting outside the show, handing out business cards and dragging people into their hotel room, Dave and Ken created some interest. They got the Deloitte & Touche and Ernst & Young reps to look at their product. Little by little, they sold single licenses for the software at about $2,000 a pop. It wasn't much, but they had a little pot of cash to afford the next trade show. In Raleigh, they also got the attention of a local investor and persuaded him to invest a few thousand dollars into Burl.

Meanwhile, Mike found his own opportunity: a struggling printing company, Marathon Typography, whose owner was willing to sell cheaply. Mike left behind his $72,000 salary at Ernst & Young and jumped into a $36,000 job as CEO and owner of the ailing printing company. Mike likes to say he "leaped with lead pants on." Marathon was losing money (sometimes Mike didn't even get his salary) because customers were switching over to the new Macintosh platform and taking their typesetting work in-house. As if that weren't enough, a week after Mike left his cushy job, his wife told him she was pregnant.

"Everyone thought I was crazy," Mike says. But Mike was happy to be free of the strictures at Ernst & Young. He'd learned the finer points of business and made a lot of contacts. Here, in the trenches at Marathon, he could try out all that he'd learned. The new Macintosh, which had an easy-to-use mouse that graphic artists could use to create amazing graphics, would eventually make Marathon's conventional typography services obsolete. Still, Mike knew that every obstacle has an opportunity, and he knew he could find it.

Mike had some awful days. Once, a customer passed him a bad check for $55,000 for some computer equipment. Mike spent a whole summer trying to collect the debt. Finally, he drove to the customer's last known address in Florida, where he found the equipment at a pawnshop. He got the equipment back and resold it to make up the debt; he even talked tough with a lawyer the customer hired to dispute the issue. Mike was going to do whatever it took to make a success of Marathon. "Failure," he says, "was never an option."

In the hills of rural New Hampshire, where Dave grew up, they have this advice for city folks who stop and ask directions: "You can't get there from here." Lost on a Sunday afternoon drive, many tourists are stumped by this advice. All it means, Dave explains, is that there's no direct route. It means you'll have to drive all the way around a lake because there's no bridge, or you'll have to go along next to the Interstate for miles because there's no entrance ramp. What those farmers know is that the city folks don't really want to get to their destination if it takes too much effort. When obstacles piled up and the going got tough, Dave, Ken, and Mike were willing to make the effort.

■ Building Momentum

Twenty-first-century hunters rarely work alone. We all have a network of allies, partners, friends, and even perfect strangers who we call on to help us reach our goals. And we can help these people in return. In fact, that's the real key to networking.

At Burl, Dave and Ken built a product that could solve some of the computing problems in corporate America. When they set out to network and tell people about it, they stopped at nothing. Their enthusiasm at trade shows was unrelenting. But folks didn't hold it against them because their product really did work. Their persistence and tenacity—and their group energy—set the stage for them to literally make millions.

The wheels started turning at their first big trade show when they met an executive from Micro Focus, a huge player in their field. He brushed them off, saying he couldn't look at their Burl Software booth because he had to set up his own booth. So they dragged him away, saying they'd set up his booth for him. The executive looked at their software. He was impressed. And Ken and Dave spent the rest of the night setting up his booth with him. They'd made a first contact.

While Ken and Dave used the usual techniques of generating interest at trade shows—handing out business cards, giving away free software, and raffling off a television—they also did the unusual. They spent hours riding shuttle buses that ferried people between trade shows and hotels, drumming up interest by pretending to be consultants who were impressed with that product at the Burl

Software booth. Another trick: They set up their booth in front of the lunch line so people would have to look at their product on their way to eat. Whatever it took, they were going to get out the word about Burl.

Their most brash move came in Disney World, where Micro Focus was holding a users group conference. Dave and Ken registered for the conference and followed the Micro Focus CEO around Pleasure Island, talking to him whenever they could. To make their company look bigger, they brought along a friend and client and had him put on a Burl badge and introduce himself to the Micro Focus CEO as an employee.

By 1995, when they had a few employees and some small investments, Dave and Ken got a call from Micro Focus that changed their lives. The British-owned company wanted to acquire them, partly because Burl was getting into an exclusive agreement with a Micro Focus competitor. The day after Micro Focus called, the pair was on a plane to London. By Monday, they had sold the company for $13.5 million.

At the same time, over at the ailing Marathon Co., Mike had found the opportunity he needed. The way he saw it, Marathon's business model was going to be extinct. So he might as well forget about the printing business and focus on the new business: in-house graphics. As companies took their graphics production in-house, they were hitting some big snags. The new Macintosh platform had trouble "talking" to the large computer networks of corporate America. Mike's solution was to morph Marathon into a totally new kind of company. He built it into a systems integration company that would help companies do a better job with the in-house graphics trend by using the Internet. But he needed some help.

So he called Dave and Ken, who had just sold Burl. Though now millionaires, Dave and Ken still loved the hunt for entrepreneurial success. So the three formed a partnership to run the new-and-improved Marathon Group. Mike could have found other technicians to write the software, but he knew Dave and Ken could do more than write code: they could think through problems.

Whenever the three friends got hold of a project, they felt they couldn't fail. At Marathon, they set out to prove that.

■ Taking the Next Leap

Dave, Mike, and Ken have an incredible synergy. At Marathon, the trio used this group energy to push their business. It's not just the ideas or the tools, it's the way each member of the group uses his strengths to enable the others to do their jobs better.

In their case, Mike is the expert on business models. The way he looks at it, all companies do two things: they make things and they sell things. At Marathon, he would study Fortune 500 companies to figure how they made and sold things. Armed with this information, he would bring in Dave and Ken, who would figure out how to make tools for the client to make and sell its product better.

Still, it wasn't just their products, it was the confidence that the three friends inspired in each other. That confidence just rubs off on other people and inspires trust. For example, Marathon was trying to elbow its way into designing Web sites for Fortune 500 firms in the late 1990s. They talked Wrangler into letting them build its on-line catalog and store locator to put on its planned Web site. In the middle of the project, the advertising agency that was designing the Wrangler site tried to scare Marathon off. So Dave, Mike, and Ken fought back together. They managed to force the agency off the project by using their own money to find another big firm to build a better Web site, presenting the superior work to Wrangler.

Wrangler was so impressed with Marathon's work that they gave Marathon the whole project. That sent the trio on a path of making e-business solutions for huge companies like Volvo, RJR, and Healthtex. In 1999, they sold Marathon Group to Merant, an Oregon-based holding company that specialized in providing custom software to some of the country's largest corporations. By now, Mike, Dave, and Ken had built amazing momentum. Their third venture was SmartPath, which produces project management software to run marketing campaigns within large companies like Wyeth, National Geographic, and Kohler. In 2004, SmartPath was acquired by DoubleClick. The three are now working together at DoubleClick.

Looking back, Dave says building a company from scratch brings to mind the Stone Soup fable. That's the story where three travelers arrive in a starving village and slip a rock into a pot of boiling water, then tell everyone they're making stone soup. One by one, the villagers donate their small portions of food: a few carrots, a hunk of cabbage, and bits of meat. Finally, there really is a delicious pot of soup for them all to share.

"In real life, it's hard to find that magic stone," Dave says. Over 14 years, this energetic trio was able to find several magic stones—or business opportunities—and turn them into businesses.

Finding that energy with the right people can mean the difference between success and failure.

■ Chapter Fifteen

Susan Flores, Founder of **Barefoot Café**

Mentors

In a day and age when great mentors are as few and far between as honest CEOs, this story shows the drastic effect a strong mentor can have on a young, impressionable businessperson. Susan Flores's strong mentors helped her leave her job and navigate the rough surf of launching a business on a nearly deserted Caribbean island.

Up at 5 AM each day to bake muffins, Susan would bicycle her way to her café and work all day long serving coffee and snacks to tourists. The space was so tiny that most of the seating was outdoors. Competition was tough on the island, which was just being built up by a resort and some enterprising small business owners. Susan made mistakes by getting into business with the wrong people and even had to hire a lawyer to get out of a bad partnership. Little by little, Susan turned problems into opportunities and kept on learning and improving.

Ten years later, the Barefoot Café is a full-fledged restaurant, and Susan has branched out to become sole coffee distributor to the now-bustling Providenciales island in the Turks and Caicos chain. Right from the beginning, her dream to start a business in the islands was different from most. Susan was serious.

Anyone who has ever vacationed in exotic places has probably thought the same thing: "Wouldn't it be nice to quit my job back home, sell everything, move here, start and run a little café, and live here for the rest of my life?" Usually, the fantasy fades as soon as we get back to work, and we don't pursue it seriously.

This wasn't the case for Susan, a Canadian public relations specialist who had her own love for traveling the Caribbean islands. She researched the islands for a year, finally settling on the remote islands of Turks and Caicos, 500 miles southeast of Miami. With hard work and tenacity, she weathered some storms and built her dream, the Barefoot Café. Susan's hard work got her where she is, but she also had the help of some amazing mentors.

Susan's first mentors were her parents, two self-employed interior decorators in suburban Toronto. While her parents worked hard, they also took plenty of time off for travel. By the time she was a teenager, she'd already had a taste of traveling to exotic locales. Susan also knew the value of work and put in long hours babysitting, cashiering at the local A&P grocery store, and managing the candy concession at a movie theater. Her bosses always commented on how she always put her heart and soul into her work. But Susan says she always knew in her bones that someday she would put even more effort into working for herself.

In college, Susan got a degree in marketing. She also took some extra courses on entrepreneurship that she thought might come in handy someday. Impatient to get into the real world, she took a heavy course load and graduated early.

Her first job was in public relations for one of the world's largest hospitality companies, Delta Hotels. She worked at a Delta hotel and conference center located directly across from the Toronto airport and was responsible for the service and promotion of its day-to-day event business. As the year wore on, she came into contact with high-level executives, wealthy business owners, and politicians. With her reserved, humble, and almost disarming demeanor, Susan quickly made friends and gained the trust of patrons.

One of her frequent clients was Robert Fennimore, a politician from Nova Scotia. Before his days in government, Robert had built a powerful international travel agency completely starting from scratch. Now in his early 60s, Robert had had his heyday in business and was consumed by his duties for the Canadian government.

As we go through our jobs each day, we often meet mentors who are willing to share with us their valuable experience about the business world. These are people who will go over our plans with us simply because it's exhilarating to watch a start-up plan hatch. Part of the entrepreneurial mind-set is to notice this network, seek out powerful people, gain their trust, and ask for their mentorship. Without her mentor, Susan may have still started her Caribbean business, but having a mentor made it a lot easier.

■ Starting from Scratch

Susan told Fennimore about her desire to find land in one of the Caribbean islands and open some sort of business that would pay the bills. Instead of laughing at the idea, Fennimore embraced it, seeing in Susan his same love for travel and an entrepreneurial mind-set, the same mind-set that breeds ownership and action. Fennimore knew travel, and he was about to give Susan some very powerful advice.

"Go on a tour," he told her. "Go on a tour of every country and island where you think you might want to work." He even gave her VIP passes through the travel company that he still owned, which made the traveling less expensive. "Go and travel, look and see where you would want to live, where you would want to run a business, and where you see the most potential. Pick the three best places to live, and we'll decide together."

After traveling to more than a dozen islands, she narrowed it down to St. Johns, Nevis, and the Turks and Caicos Islands. With Fennimore's help, Susan chose Turks and Caicos. It was only a three-and-a-half-hour flight from Toronto, its official language was

English, and a developer was breaking ground on a retail shopping center. I recently spent some time in the Turks and Caicos Islands, and there are still only a few small flights a day, a one-landing-strip airport, one hotel, a few gorgeous condominium buildings, two grocery stores, and only a few dozen restaurants. When Susan chose Turks and Caicos as her destination, there was less than that, and the place was a complete mystery to most people in the United States. Turks and Caicos was almost all potential and very little existing business.

Besides potential, the Turks and Caicos Islands had another thing going for it: it had one of the few island governments that allowed nonresidents to purchase a business license.

Although Susan had no money and still owed on student loans, another mentor came to her aid: her grandfather had retired with a small amount of retirement savings, around $40,000. "Gramps" had the confidence to loan Susan the money to bootstrap her business idea.

One of her first decisions was also the most important. Susan decided to lease her location instead of building and owning a shop. Fennimore told her it was good to lease because "if it doesn't go well, you're not invested too deeply." Over the years, as Turks and Caicos Islands built up, Susan saw a lot of business owners get in over their heads with high start-up costs and then go out of business. She decided to keep her costs low, and that ended up making all the difference.

Susan likes to say she prospered the old-fashioned way, through plenty of hard work. She would wake before dawn to bake muffins, load them onto her bicycle, and pedal to work. At the café, she got things ready for her first customers and worked all through the day. "When it got busy it was overwhelming," she says. In those early days she was bone-tired, putting her heart and soul into building her business. When a former coworker from Delta said she'd like to go in as a partner, Susan gladly agreed. That's when Susan learned her difficult lesson about partnerships.

■ Underestimating Obstacles

"We weren't on the same track," Susan says of her first business partner, who nearly smashed her Caribbean dream. While Susan would work from dawn till dark, her business partner was lazy and in love and her mind was elsewhere.

This was terrible. Wanting to be fair, Susan had drawn up the partnership papers to say that they owned the business 50-50, even though Susan had more money invested. After a few weeks, Susan wanted out and proposed to buy the partner out. Maybe it was a case of hurt feelings, but the business partner was intransigent. She left and wouldn't deal with the problem, leaving Susan to figure out a remedy.

Despite that problem, the little café did a good business. Susan single-handedly prepared and served the food, getting "swamped" in the lunchtime rush. Sometimes she had part-time help, but mostly she just worked fast.

Susan ended up flying to the government center on Grand Turk Island and dissolving the partnership. Since her partner wouldn't agree to let Susan buy her out or any other reasonable option, her mentor advised Susan to close the business to sever all business ties with the woman. Susan had to convince the government she was starting a new business. She sold the furnishings, changed the interior decor, painted the walls a different color, and changed the name from Island Dream to Barefoot Café.

A month later, under her own name with no partner, Susan bought back the furnishings, resigned her leases, and opened back up. Gramps even gave her some more money and told her to only pay interest until she had cash. Bruised from the experience, Susan was determined to make her mentors proud. She went back to work and tried again.

Business was good, so Susan expanded her menu to include ham and turkey sandwiches and eggs, which she cooked on two little hot plates. The Barefoot Café was turning out to be a gold mine because she'd kept her costs low. Susan made 50 cents on every dollar she took in.

Then one day, Susan came to work to find a situation every entrepreneur dreads. Her brisk business had caught the attention of someone with deep pockets who set up a big restaurant with a full kitchen and complete line of deli meats right next door. All Susan had was two lunch meats, muffins, and two hot plates. "For sure, I thought she was going to put me out of business," Susan recalls. Then Susan found out that even though she had opened up first, the competitor had gotten from the landlord exclusive rights to a deli in the shopping center.

In the end, it was Susan's decision to keep costs down that saved her. Barefoot Café was profitable from the start, but the new restaurant, with its high start-up costs and overhead, couldn't keep up and closed within six months. Her landlord came to her and said, "You're way too busy; this little space isn't big enough for you." So Susan moved into the bigger space. This time, she got a clause in the lease giving her exclusive rights to use the courtyard—and she would be the only restaurant in the shopping center.

■ Building Momentum

On an island, friendships form fast. During her early, frenzied days in her first, smaller café, Susan got to know a woman who was visiting the island. She helped Susan make sandwiches during the lunch rush and confessed to Susan that she also had a dream of starting a business in Turks and Caicos. Remembering her mentor's help, Susan decided to do the woman a good turn and offered to help finance the new business in return for a few things.

Susan and her friend came up with a plan. Susan would loan her money to rent the retail shop next door for a clothing store. In return, the friend would allow the Barefoot Café to set up tables outside. And the friend would shut down at lunchtime and help Susan make sandwiches. The deal worked out well for both of them.

Another business alliance Susan forged had to do with coffee. In the coffee business, a retailer contracts with a roaster to process its coffee beans. Early on, Susan found a premium roaster to do business with and came up with her own "Barefoot Blend." On an island where the grocery stores sometimes ran out of milk before the next shipment flew in, having a dependable coffee supplier was crucial.

Thanks to her Barefoot Blend coffee, the café built a loyal following among tourists, Club Med employees, and construction workers. They all flocked to her little café for that special Barefoot Blend coffee and a bite to eat. When lunch crowds overwhelmed the little café, regulars would pitch in and help.

Pretty soon, the other restaurants, resorts, and hotels on the island were coming to Susan for coffee advice. Coffee is the second largest exported commodity in the world next to oil. The world of specialty coffees is a complex system where the best coffee beans are sold by brokers who negotiate prices with buyers all over the world. Susan learned the system and bought the top quality from all over the world. Then her roaster processed them and shipped them to her. Eventually, Susan became a coffee distributor with exclusive rights to the Providenciales Island.

Susan's entrepreneurial mind-set and help from mentors saw her through rough times to sunny skies. From the first year, even with her legal troubles, she has been profitable. Thanks to her grandfather's loans, she wasn't burdened with debt and in the beginning only paid interest. After a few years, she paid back her grandfather everything. And she's kept her eyes out for other opportunities, investing in the retail clothing business next door, buying real estate, and growing her own business.

There were other partnerships as well. Susan's love of soccer led to a friendship with the activities director for a nearby resort. She would watch him play soccer, he would come over to the café for ice cream, and they would talk. The pair started a teenage girl's hockey league and a deep friendship grew. After a few years, they married and left the island for a few years to raise their children in Canada, entrusting the Barefoot Café to a manager.

■ Taking the Next Leap

Running a business long distance is hard. Susan ran the Barefoot Café from Canada for three years using a string of managers. The business did well under the hired managers but not great. Nobody runs a business as well as an owner. In 2005, Susan found a buyer for the café and sold it for what she calls a fantastic profit.

The coffee distributorship is another story. It's the kind of business that can scale up as customers are added along the way. Now she and her husband talk about distributing coffee to other vacation hotspots around the world. Wherever they decide to go, they want luxurious beaches and access to an airport so that they can visit family. What a life!

She and her husband also plan to teach their children about business from a very young age. Already they plan to set up the kids with their own small businesses doing whatever they love while they're just teenagers. That way, they can make their mistakes early. "If they don't do well, we'll be there," Susan says. "So when they go out to the real world they will be prepared." She's hopeful the entrepreneurship gene has been passed on to the next generation.

Like so many of the ordinary people in this book, Susan has completely mastered the art of the HUNT and has several powerful secrets to share. What stands out in her story are her powerful mentors, who continued to keep the young entrepreneur on the right track and helped her deal with some troubles along the way. And Susan has returned the favor and mentored other aspiring entrepreneurs along the way.

Her advice to those who want to set up shop in vacation spots like the Caribbean islands is to do it. Today. Before you decide where, visit the location, sit down and watch it all day, and see where the sun shines, where the afternoon shadows fall. Think it through and then do it. Find a business you enjoy, she says, and learn the laws of the island.

Even though she got in the Turks and Caicos Islands early, she says new businesses open up there and prosper. While it may have been cheaper ten years ago, credit is also easier to get nowadays, Susan points out.

And even if your dream isn't to go to an island, Susan's story of hard work and mentorship is inspiring. It just goes to show that a little guidance can go a long way.

■ Chapter Sixteen

Tim O'Leary, Founder of **Respond2 Communications, Inc.**   ■

Communicate

Do you remember the NordicTrack infomercials? Well, Tim O'Leary is the guy who started it all, the modern infomercial as we know it. If you've ever wanted to know about advertising and the media industry, this story is for you. O'Leary's humble beginnings began selling out of a beat-up pickup truck. Now you probably see one of his commercials every time you turn on the TV. Whether you love infomercials or not, they represent the vibrant, fast-growing field of direct-response advertising.

Success—followed fast by failure—came early to Tim. First, he started a computer company and failed; then he sold gas pumps and got bored. Finally, he started to hunt after his dreams. Now, at age 45, he's an infomercial guru and CEO of his own company, Respond2 Communications.

At first, Tim felt invincible. In high school, he was a debate team champion; in college, he was an advertising whiz kid with a campus job promoting rock concerts and rubbing shoulders with rock stars, picking them up at the airport and showing them around town.

Then he made some cash in college when he put together a clever little TV ad for one of his dad's friends. The ad was for the

"Tak Pak," a chest-mounted tackle box fishermen could wear while they were wading in streams. The inventor was a fishing guide who had worked for the *Wide World of Sports* whenever it came through Montana. The guy had film footage of famous folks, like Jimmy Carter, wearing the Tak Pak and wading in streams. Tim took that footage, turned it into a commercial, and ran it on latenight TV; it made him thousands of dollars—which was good money in the early 1980s. He graduated from college cocksure and confident that he would make his mark on LA's glitzy advertising world.

Instead, Tim found out he hated Los Angeles and figured he wasn't cut out to be an ad executive. He returned to Montana, came up with a great idea for a computer business, and struck it rich for a couple years. Tim likes to say he was terribly arrogant, "until he learned how easy it is to fail." When his business failed—fast and hard—Tim went back to working for his dad. That's how he ended up driving around selling gas pumps.

One day, driving around rural Montana, Tim realized life was too short to spend hating his job. He drove to the nearest big city— Portland, Oregon—got an apartment, and started meeting the local TV production folks. Somehow, he knew he would find a way to cobble together a career that had something to do with his first love: TV advertising.

When Tim tells his story, he talks in a loud, clear voice with al- most no pauses. One sentence marches on to the next, and he's never at a loss for what to say. That's no accident. As a kid, he'd looked up to his father as a great salesman. But despite his great sales talents when he spoke to people, his dad froze whenever he saw a microphone, and Tim vowed that he would learn from the great speechmakers he watched on TV, like John F. Kennedy and Martin Luther King, Jr. Through all the ups and downs of his career, Tim still thinks that his ability to speak in front of people is what serves him best.

Another thing he'd learned in school was that even though he had acted in commercials, his favorite part about advertising was being the boss. "I just wanted to own companies," Tim says.

So when Tim started hanging around Portland's production businesses, he was looking for a company to start. What he found were two producers, an editor, and a director making corporate films and commercials out of a house. They called themselves Tyee Productions, and they had a lot of creativity and were doing great work, but they had minimal business experience and no real marketing effort behind them. They also couldn't afford to pay him much. Tim said that was fine, to just give him a small salary, and he'd work on commission for all the sales he brought in. They agreed, and he dug in to figure out the business.

Finally, Tim was having fun.

■ Starting from Scratch

Even though he was only 30 years old when he joined Tyee, Tim felt older because he'd already been through several start-ups.

His first starting-from-scratch story had nothing to do with TV, and maybe that's why it failed. Tim's first company, Cork Control, made a computer system for gas stations—it started when he first started selling gas pumps after he decided he didn't like LA. Driving through the rural West, Tim was fascinated with the new payment cards. The primitive technology didn't even use magnetic cards; instead, it had an optical card reader. "I thought 'this is cool, I want to sell these,'" Tim recalls. The gadgets weren't catching on because they would spit out complicated financial reports, and gas station operators just couldn't understand them. Tim made an effort to understand.

Back then, the only small computers were Apples. So Tim borrowed money from his father to buy an Apple and then hired a guy to write a software program to translate the optical card reader's financial report into an understandable accounting format. The gadget allowed gas stations in rural areas to have self-serve pumps that could sell gas without attendants 24 hours a day, seven days a week. Twenty-five years ago, that was a unique concept. "I started selling card systems like crazy," Tim recalls.

At that point, he was 24 years old and had thrown together a company that he had no idea how to run. Tim knew how to spend money, though, and bought himself a Porsche and a house. What he didn't spend money on was research and development; when IBM announced its new PC, Tim's business fell hard. Customers called to say they wanted his software, but they wanted the system on a PC. It would have taken Tim two years to hire a developer to do that. Unlike Dave Babson (Chapter 14), Tim hadn't built a core group of people with programming and business expertise. Also, Tim says he should have set aside cash; he should have gone out and forged relationships with hardware manufacturers; and he should have looked for investors. "But I was pretty much just out there on my own," Tim recalls, and to add insult to injury, he felt like a lot of people in town enjoyed seeing him flame out. "After all, nobody wants to see a 24-year-old smart-ass make it."

The second time around, when 30-year-old Tim was joining Tyee Productions, he was careful with money and avoided debt. No more Porsches for a while. And instead of just selling commercials and making money, he was thinking about how to build a solid company.

One thing Tyee had already done before Tim got there was an infomercial for Soloflex, a $1,200 exercise machine that became a cultural phenomenon. Back then, and even now, most infomercials use a "yell and sell" format. But Tyee's Soloflex infomercial was a highly produced little story about a guy who works out on his So-loflex machine in his classy loft and on weekends goes off to play touch football with some friends. When he strips off his shirt on the field, everyone is staring at his rippling muscles. It was very sexy.

Before Tim joined the company, Tyee had produced the info-mercial for a flat fee; and now Soloflex was making millions of dol-lars in sales from that one infomercial. Tim was determined to get another chance for Tyee to produce another exercise infomercial, but this time the company would be compensated better. Looking through the back of a magazine, Tim found an ad for an exercise equipment maker—NordicTrack—and gave the company a call. They'd seen the Soloflex infomercial and were looking for an expert to help them create something like it. Tim said he was an expert— after all, Tyee had produced the Soloflex piece—and made an appointment to meet with NordicTrack soon. The only problem was that he still wasn't sure how to structure the deal so Tyee would get a fair price.

■ Underestimating Obstacles

In the late 1980s, infomercials were something new. They'd only just become legal in 1985, thanks to an FCC ruling that took away limits on the length of TV ads. They were so new that Tim hadn't learned about them in college.

Tim started learning fast. Even though the failure with his first company made him cautious about money, he was still good at underestimating obstacles. He only had a few weeks to figure out the infomercial business, but he was willing to try. Plus he was lucky. There was an infomercial trade group forming and holding its first meeting in Las Vegas. Tyee had no travel budget and it was an 18-hour drive. Here's where the lessons of the past came in: Tim drove to the conference for the price of gas. No flights for him. He could underestimate obstacles, but he wasn't careless with money.

Tim was shocked by what he saw at the meeting. Here was a multi-million-dollar industry, and many of the people making and selling infomercials looked like "charlatans and freaks," as Tim says. But they were making money by producing cheap, low-quality infomercials. "If they can make money," Tim thought, "what would happen if someone good and reputable came into the business?"

Besides looking better, Tyee's infomercials could turn the business on its ear. While the low-budget "scream and sell" infomercials got sales results, top brands weren't buying them, afraid they would hurt their image. At the time, infomercial producers were charging only about $100,000 plus a percentage of the gross sales. Since the products were inexpensive things—kitchen gadgets and cleaning products—those sales figures didn't amount to a lot. If Tyee produced quality infomercials—but charged more up front— perhaps it could convince corporate America to run them for higher-priced items like household electronics and exercise equipment.

All he had to do was convince NordicTrack.

Tim built his strategy around the idea that spending a lot of money on a great TV infomercial would drive sales in a way that a cheap ad couldn't. Growing up around small businesses, Tim knew that any businessperson hated waste, especially when it came to advertising. Every dollar counted. At an early age, Tim's father taught him to read a financial statement, so he was at ease building up a presentation about cost ratios. He could explain how a good infomercial would give NordicTrack a three-to-one profit ratio on its media spending. For example, for every dollar spent on airtime, the company should get at least three dollars in sales. A good ad could do this.

Tim had all his figures straight, plus he had another skill: when he made a presentation, he owned the room.

■ Building Momentum

Tim was back in his element. Instead of selling gas pumps or computers, he was selling something he knew: TV advertising.

Tim knew TV like I know financial planning; he'd hung around a television station all through college and even acted in commercials in a pinch. He was so relaxed speaking in public that he had a college gig as a movie critic at a Montana TV station. Hanging around that TV station, he'd learned things about advertising that most people didn't know. Plus, whenever he came up against something he didn't understand, he had a great network to consult with.

Thanks to his network of TV contacts, Tim knew about the more obscure kinds of advertising tactics, such as "per inquiry" (PI). That's when a TV station gives its commercial slots away for free in return for a percentage of each product sold. Sure, it's not the best airtime, usually late at night or early in the morning, but it's a way to sell things. For instance, a company with an inexpensive item could run its ads for free, sell its gadgets for $40 each, and let the station keep $20. PI advertising was a common tool in the early days of cable TV, especially for new stations that had a lot of unsold ad slots. It's not nearly so common today.

Tim's TV expertise wowed the NordicTrack people. Their first contract with Tyee was for three shows in three months. It was a tight production schedule, but Tyee could hustle.

The first NordicTrack show surpassed all expectations with a staggering $300 million in sales. To this day, Tim still remembers that figure. And he remembers how NordicTrack's stock went through the roof just after the company had become a publicly traded company. It also put Tyee on the map.

Tyee started to get a reputation as an expensive company for doing infomercials—but also one of the best. Instead of charging $100,000 for a cheesy infomercial, as most companies did, Tyee charged $300,000 to $600,000 per show. That gave the necessary cash flow to build a company infrastructure. Tim knew what it was like not to have enough money to deal with competition—that's what had happened in his computer business. So he took the money and attracted great infomercial talent.

His strategy worked. Nicer infomercials attracted a nicer clientele, and Tyee started to attract big names like AT&T, Sony, Toshiba, and Philips. Established brands started to use infomercials as a way to introduce new products to consumers. Yet, even with that high-priced reputation, Tim remembered not to get carried away.

First and foremost, the point of the infomercials was to drive sales—not to be flashy. With lessons from his previous ventures in mind, he always positioned Tyee as expensive but able to generate great sales.

It's always good to think about where you want to go. And Tim was thinking. In the back of his mind, he had an exit strategy. He wanted to build a great company that someday could be sold. Having a lot of working capital was a great way to do this.

■ Taking the Next Leap

As Tyee evolved, Tim's position with the original three owners changed. Instead of continuing to work for a salary, he formed his own company in partnership with them—TV Tyee—that would be the creative sales arm. He would act as agent for Tyee Productions and pay them to make infomercials. The other owners still had an ownership position, but Tim kept the controlling interest.

While Tyee was mainly about productions, Tim had a new business model in mind and wanted to branch out into other things. Production was nice, but he figured the big money was in consulting services, where he could use his advertising expertise to put together whole strategies. Tyee always did the producing for him.

Fear of debt provided the other reason why Tim set up this structure. After his spending binge with his first company, he wanted to build the business slowly and not take on debt. But the Tyee people wanted to buy expensive new editing suites on credit. After what he'd gone through in his 20s, he didn't want any part of that. Instead, Tim wanted great cash flow and to make a lot of money personally to invest for the future. By separating production and consulting, he could distance himself from his partners' debts.

The 1990s were great for TV Tyee. When Philips's first DVD player came out, it introduced the product through Tyee infomercials. The same for Sony surround sound, Web TV, and big-screen televisions. Tyee even did the Sears ads with home repair guru Bob Villa. Instead of churning out infomercials for get-rich-quick schemes, skin care, and real estate books, Tyee was competing with mainstream advertising on respected products. Tyee kept raising its price because it was the only game in town, charging up to $1 million per campaign, with companies lining up to pay.

With things growing so fast, Tim's company and Tyee merged into the Tyee Group. But just when things were flying high, tensions between the partners started to drag it down. From Tim's point of view, big money was blinding his partners to sensible business practices. He couldn't stand seeing money wasted and rash business decisions made. "It's like ordering a steak, taking one bite, and throwing it away," he says. Plus, his partners wanted to sell out to a bigger advertising agency right away; Tim wanted to wait until Tyee grew more.

That's when the next phase of Tim's career started. After 10 years with Tyee, the partners bought Tim out in the late 1990s, giving him half his share up front and the rest over time. By now, he was a wealthy man who didn't have to work but loved the game of advertising. He took a year off and married Michelle Cardinal (who he met on the NordicTrack deal), someone who loved the advertising industry as much as he did. Together, they launched a new company, and now they each run their own company side-by-side out of a rehabbed dairy building in Portland. Tim's company, Respond2, produces infomercials. Michelle's company, Cmedia, holds inventory and manages sales—pricing items, buying airtime, doing telemarketing, and fulfilling orders.

Together, they get the word out to consumers about products like Johnny Carson DVDs, KitchenAid products, Stanley tools, and the Songbird hearing aid. Between them they gross about $110 million annually and plan to build things bigger before selling to a large agency or going public.

It's a long way from selling gas pumps—and it's all thanks to Tim's early talent for communication.

PART 4

Take the First Step

Isaac Newton figured this out long ago: An object at rest tends to stay at rest; an object in motion tends to stay in motion. Are you an object in motion? Or are you an object at rest? If you're at rest and in a rut, you need to work on the final and all-important step of the HUNT. The T, taking the first step, will help you overcome your inertia and stagnation to put you on the path to a better career and a better life.

While the HUNT begins with harnessing what you have, underestimating your obstacles, and noticing your network, each of those actions requires taking steps. Sitting down and assessing your strengths is a step; being optimistic about your chances of starting a business is a step; and calling friends and telling them about your plans is a step. Each day you can take one small step to build some momentum. Consider this: the journey of a thousand miles begins with one step.

Most of us avoid first steps because we tend to resist and avoid change. This happens every day. We start to do something or think of a project, then immediately in our heads we start making excuses why we shouldn't. We talk ourselves out of going to a networking meeting because we don't think we'll meet anyone of value when we get there. We talk ourselves out of making a phone call to ask advice because we don't think the person on the other line will be interested. We talk ourselves out of going to the gym because it'll be too crowded. As a general rule of thumb: If you find yourself *trying* to talk yourself out of something, chances are you should make it happen. The only hunter who is sure of going hungry is the one who doesn't go on the hunt.

Maybe you're not stagnant—you're moving along at a fast pace—but you're exhausted and dissatisfied. You could be moving full speed ahead in the wrong direction. That's where the other part of Newton's Law of Inertia comes in: An object in motion will continue to move in a straight line unless acted upon by another force. Because humans are resistant to change, we would rather stay on the wrong path than change course to a new unknown. Often it's because we're too proud to change direction.

Whether you're stagnant or going in the wrong direction, the HUNT can help you get moving in the right direction. By harnessing what you have, underestimating your obstacles, and noticing your network, you can get everything in line with the right road map to your future. All you need is to provide yourself with a catalyst to take the first step. Success comes from your ability to listen to the voice inside you calling for change. The first action is the hardest, but once you push the first stone it can be the start of a landslide. Dave Babson (Chapter 14) says "the effort of going from zero to one feels infinite," but once you get to the first step, it's much easier to get to steps two, three, four, and five. You owe it to yourself to start your own landslide today, so start working on going from step zero to step one.

What I'm NOT talking about is an all-or-nothing approach. I'm talking about pushing one pebble over the edge. All 21 of the ordinary people in this book took first steps in a variety of forms: sitting down to write a list, taking an entrepreneurship class, or making a prototype for a new product. After a few first steps, the domino effect kicks in. If you're dissatisfied in your place in life, take a chance and see where it leads you.

Last year I was lucky enough to be able to spend some time with Rudy Giuliani in his office overlooking Manhattan. At the top edge of his mahogany desk sat a large marble engraving that read "I'm responsible." I will take the weight and meaning of that to my grave. That's a powerful statement, especially coming from the man who presided over New York City following 9/11. It means you're the only person who is going to make something happen for yourself—not your mother, not your father, and not your friends.

People who master the art of the HUNT are people like you who take dissatisfaction as a signal to take a new first step in a different direction. Often you don't know where that first step will lead you—but that's the point. If you feel like you're in a dry and barren pond where you are seldom rewarded for your talents and rarely given credit for your unique contribution, taking the first step will provide you a new direction. Corporate America can be a great place to build wealth; however, not every big corporation is financially able to take care of you for your whole life. Remember, it's not personal; it's just business. If you cost a corporation money— today, tomorrow, five years, or ten years from now—you'll be forced to take a step. So why not take a step while you still have a choice?

A first step can be just one inch. Every single person in this book got to their goal by taking first steps. And there are several examples that are more striking than others.

Notice the first steps of the people in this next section; each of them had a different approach to changing inertia in the wrong direction. Each of them got moving in their own way, with their own secret:

- **Surrounding support.** Jen Velarde wanted to be one of those people with a passion for her job, but she wasn't enjoying interior design. She found her real passion when friends and family surrounded her with support for her sewing efforts. Her first steps led her to a business that revolutionized the handbag industry.

- **Live your brand.** Kimberly Wilson felt a major gap in her life, so she decided to make small changes in her daily routine. One change was taking a yoga class; she liked it so much that she went from being yoga student to yoga teacher. After six months, she saw her path: build a brand around helping people get out of ruts and make changes. Once Kimberly got in motion, she stayed in motion.

- **Patience.** Willa Levin—one of the many thousands of overworked, underpaid, underappreciated, and overstressed nurses—set a compelling example for those stuck on 12-hour night shifts. Willa patiently worked at her career for 15 years, gaining valuable skills along the way, until one day she took one class about business that changed the course of her life forever.

- **Balance.** Jen Klair was dissatisfied with the all-or-nothing career path and wanted to find a balance between a fulfilling career and raising her family. She had absolutely no idea how to sell on the Internet, but by taking a series of small first steps she created a virtual children's blanket empire in her living room.

- **Tireless energy.** Giovanni The Margarita King (he had his name legally changed) is a man who knows nothing *but* taking first steps. He set out to open his own restaurant, then sold it, started a new one, and then continued tirelessly taking first steps that led him to a brilliant new liquor concern.

Here's the good news: What you're doing right now can be a very effective, powerful, and life-changing first step. Think of this book as a "Guide to Get Going." Many of the wildly successful people in this book—Maria Churchill, Jen Klair, Kimberly Wilson, Warren Brown, Matt Lindner, and Tim O'Leary—did the same thing you're doing right now: they read books about purposes, direction, business, and self-discovery.

You're almost there. The HUNT rises and falls on taking first steps, and the only sure way to fail is by *not* taking steps or moving forward. Will Rogers said: "Even if you're on the right track, you'll get run over if you just sit there." Whether it's a radical career change or a small change in your daily routine, you're on your way already. Keep going and find the inspiration to take the first step.

■ Chapter Seventeen

Jen Velarde, Founder of **1154 LILL**

Surrounding Support

Attention ladies and fashion-forward types: If Maria Churchill's story about starting Debout Shoes didn't quite fit your fantasy, then prepare to read about your dream job.

Jen Velarde combined a career she didn't like with some fabric samples nobody wanted and sewed up her own handbag empire. Spurred on by people who loved their jobs—and people who wanted her to love hers—Jen created 1154 LILL, a brand with three boutiques, a popular Web site, and a sprawling nationwide program that gathers neighborhood women together for revelry and custom handbag shopping.

It all started with a feeling in the pit of her stomach. Remember the Sunday night blues? Jen had studied four years in college for her design degree, and yet when she got her first job, she knew it wasn't for her. Designing office spaces just wasn't what she thought it would be. Instead of picking out fabrics and textures and talking with excited clients, she was sitting through endless meetings and living on the road visiting companies. She was miserable.

"You know when you see people who have found their groove?" says Jen. She resolved to be one of those people.

Like a lot of us with college degrees, Jen wasn't really prepared to apply her talents to the working world. Instead, her education had prepared her to fit into a job working for a larger organization. Her story of searching from job to job is one a lot of people can relate to.

Her first job in the mid-1990s was designing office furniture for a large furniture company in Iowa. With the pressure to find a job right after college, Jen felt lucky to have a job at all, even if it was one she didn't love. In desperation, she'd considered graphic arts— which wasn't her specialty—or even sales, anything that would draw a paycheck. Looking back, she wishes maybe she'd waited a little longer and taken time to think about it.

As it happened, that first job got her foot in the door, and a year later she was designing corporate offices for a small Chicago firm. It was a great place to work, but she still didn't love it. She put in a lot of hours and wasn't getting a lot of satisfaction. "At the end of the day, I didn't feel like I was connected to the projects or connected to the clients," Jen says. When she thinks back on it, those early years are fuzzy and gray because she was working just for a paycheck.

Finally, Jen moved to a larger firm, Space, that was doing edgier corporate designs. Jen connected with a senior designer there, and the two put together a model of a new three-story office space with a beautiful two-story glass atrium and colorful fabrics. The project was for an advertising agency that was moving from traditional offices full of perpendicular halls and closed rooms to an open floor plan with curves and invigorating open areas for collaboration. It was a fun project, but the best part about it was the head designer's enthusiasm for her job. After that project ended, so did the collaboration. And Jen was back to feeling dissatisfied. She'd taken that job with the idea that she was giving interior design one more shot. What she found was that interior design wasn't for her.

But there was a bright side: After watching the senior designer who loved her job, Jen was inspired to find work that made her jump out of bed each morning. That's when she started hunting for great work.

■ Starting from Scratch

It's amazing how much a little encouragement can mean along the way.

Jen was on the road all of the time, and her friends and family encouraged her to use the time to take stock of her life. At that point she was 24 and earning about $30,000 a year. Sitting alone in her hotel room, Jen would think about the things that led her to choose design: her love of bright colors, crafts, and sewing projects. She used to love art class, even just hanging out in rooms full of art supplies. These were happy memories, but they didn't seem like the makings of a career. Then one night sitting in her hotel room, Jen had an inspiration to sew something. As the only girl in her family, she had great memories of special times spent sewing with her grandmother and mother. When she got home to Chicago, Jen pulled out her old sewing machine and made a purse out of some scraps.

Her first project was a small green chenille handbag with black trim and a hook closure. It wasn't a great handbag, but she'd had fun making it. "I was so excited about it, that's all that really mattered," Jen says. "I would carry it around and people would compliment me." Looking at that handbag now, Jen has to laugh at the low level of quality and workmanship. But her family and friends weren't critiquing the bag they were applauding her for doing something that made her happy.

For Jen, making that purse struck a chord in her. She kept on making purses from the piles of old fabric swatches that designers end up collecting—little pieces of fabric that weren't big enough to make much besides handbags and change purses. She loved trying different color and texture combinations, making some of the bags reversible with ribbon ties or reversible zippers. There was a lot of trial and error. For example, if you want a bag to be reversible, the stitches can't show on the inside—it's a challenge to design something like that. But Jen didn't mind hard work, not when she could turn a scrap into something usable and eye-catching. Once she started, she couldn't stop.

A great beginning isn't about things running smoothly without a hitch. In Jen's case, her beginning hit a lot of snags. After she went on a handbag-sewing frenzy, she figured she might as well sell her prototypes at a Chicago street fair. At first, it really didn't go very well. For one thing, she hadn't had time to sew enough handbags and showed up with only about 20 different bags. For another thing, it was in a different part of town than she had first thought.

But it was a beautiful day for a street fair, and her friends and family were cheering her on. She couldn't quit now. Instead, she thought on her feet. Even though it was a less than ideal location, it was a beautiful day and there was room for her to set up a table and display her paltry stock and fabric samples. As people came by to touch the colorful bags, she started her pitch: pick the style you like, then pick some fabric, and in four weeks I'll send you your finished bag. Jen also made another crucial decision: she asked people to pay her up front.

Custom-made bags were a new business model for Jen and came as a solution to her problem of not having enough stock. All day long, people flocked to Jen's table to hand over their money and order a bag in a fabric and style of their own choosing. It turned out people loved that they could have a product they designed themselves; and the price of $30 to $60 was less than they would pay for a ready-made designer bag. Jen knew she was doing a good business but didn't have a chance to count her money. At the end of the day, she had brought in $2,200. She still remembers the exact figure today without looking it up.

The next day, Jen decided that she would work toward building a business around custom-made handbags. Her parents and friends encouraged her.

She knew that if she were going to do this as a business, she ought to brand it with a recognizable label. So she chose the name 1154 LILL, after the address of the condo where she was living at the time. That address was the place where she made her first handbag, and it meant so many things to Jen: her first time living alone and her first step toward independence. As a business, 1154 LILL would liberate Jen from a so-so career and give her work that she looked forward to each day.

■ Underestimating Obstacles

The day after her successful street fair sale, Jen knew in her heart that she would sell custom-made handbags full-time. But she didn't jump right in. Like so many other entrepreneurs, Jen kept her day job. She talked to her boss and decided she could work three days a week. In her office designs, Jen always liked pushing the envelope; but in business, she wanted to play it safe. Her father, who had worked his entire career at one company, advised her to be sure to take care of details like insurance and cash reserves. It was good advice.

Jen's experience shows the value of surrounding yourself with supportive people. Her parents, her boss, and her friends all had great things to say about her new venture. Looking back, she wonders if sometimes they didn't even believe it themselves. "It took a while for people to believe it was a real business and that I wasn't sitting home having fun, enjoying the weather," Jen says. "On sunny days, they would comment on how lucky I was. They really didn't get it."

But the support was helpful, especially when Jen had her own doubts. Entrepreneurs are only human, and human beings need support. If you don't think people around you are going to support your venture, find those who will. Supportive words are like fertilizer for a new, fragile business.

In those early days, Jen found a lot of support from a friend who wanted to go the distance with her. Robin Newberry, a college friend and sorority sister, lived just down the street from her. Robin would go to handbag parties with Jen in the early days when she was still working part-time. There were some rough days, like the time Jen had to run her first handbag party on crutches because she'd broken her foot. As she stood on crutches juggling her products, Jen felt comical and not at all glamorous and independent. But even on crutches, she sold $600 worth of purses. It was enough. She figured if she could just keep selling at least that much—once or twice a week—she could think about quitting her job. "If it didn't work out, I could always go back to my job," Jen says. "I figured if I didn't try it, I would always wonder what would have happened."

Just when things were looking good, Jen had a devastating experience. The thing about being a self-made businessperson is that you have yourself to thank for successes—and yourself to blame for mistakes. As Jen describes it: "The highs are higher, and the lows are lower." For Jen, her first dissatisfied customer made her feel like a failure. The problem was a bag that she'd sold at her first street fair. Made of a pretty green fabric, the handbag had just fallen apart after just a little bit of wear. Jen wondered, "Is the phone going to keep ringing? Are people going to call and say, This is horrible; I can't believe you sold this to me!'"

For a little while, Jen was very upset. She refunded the customer's money and made her a new bag. It turned out the original fabric just wasn't sturdy enough (she had one other complaint about a bag made with the same fabric). After a few days, Jen realized that disappointments would come up, mistakes would be made. She resolved to do everything she could to ensure quality. In the end, it made her a little more realistic about having her own business: 1154 LILL wasn't going to be a party—it was work.

Another thing: Jen took her feelings of failure and did something about them. She apologized profusely to the customer and even hand-delivered the new bag to the customer's doorstep. The payback came when she saw how happy the woman was to get the new bag. It helped Jen feel she wasn't a failure—she just suffered from a case of the wrong fabric.

◼ Building Momentum

Throughout the summer of 1999, Jen along with her friend Robin, who had a full-time job, would do as many home and office parties as they could. To meet the sewing demand, she contracted people to sew the purses—but Jen always had the purses delivered to her for one last quality inspection before shipping them out.

By 2000, Jen had moved into her commercial space. During the day it was a retail store, and by night it was a location for in-store parties. Gradually, she put her energy into the in-store business and the home parties dwindled. In 2001, she moved into a better retail space. Then, people in Chicago started talking about 1154 LILL. Women would walk around with an eye-catching handbag and other women would ask them where they got it. Customers would even hand out her cards to friends and strangers. Those LILL bags became conversation starters. Newspapers wrote articles about the custom-made bags, and Jen's store was featured on the *Style Network* and a dating show.

Jen's whimsical idea to just "sit down and sew something" had turned into a full-fledged business that filled a niche. Besides her loyal Chicago following, there were out-of-town customers who bought from her Web site. Jen noticed she had a fair number of out-of-towners in Boston and Kansas City—and that gave her an idea. Since she had friends in Boston and family in the Kansas City area, Jen decided it was time to expand. In March 2004, after months of consulting with her Boston contacts and looking at properties, Jen added a Boston store. She had to personally guarantee the two-year lease, which was a risk. But it paid off. Later that year, she added a Kansas City store, with a five-year lease on a property.

On 1154 LILL's Web site, there's a photo of Jen and a bunch of smiling women who work in her store. If you think they look a little like a bunch of sorority sisters lined up for a group photo, that's no accident. Early on, Jen realized that the appeal of her store was that she was selling people a shopping experience. They come to the store—or home party—and enjoy working with the sales staff (or stylists) as they pull out fabric swatches and hold them up to get an idea of what the finished product will be like. Together, they "ooh and aah" over the fabric combinations. Later, when the customer gets her finished bag, it's like she's carrying around that warm, supportive experience from the store.

"If a customer has a good experience, she's going to talk about it," Jen says. The idea is for a customer to walk in the store and have fun—and it makes a difference when the women who work in the store look like they're having fun and enjoying themselves, Jen says. It rubs off on the customers. That's why she pays a lot of attention to the people she hires. From day one, most of the employees were friends of friends. Since most of the employees have a history with each other outside of work, it makes 1154 LILL a fun kind of place to hang out. Jen found managing her store staff was a little like playing on her high school soccer team: everyone contributes to a win. She even calls all her staff members "teammates." Jen's right-hand employee is her old college friend Robin, who was so supportive in the early days. Robin eventually quit her corporate job and came to work with Jen as her business manager.

The purse styles also became like old friends. At first, each style just had a number. But after a while, Jen started naming them: Ally, Kimberly, Liz, and Erika. She uses names of friends around the country who have supported her in some way. Between the purse names and the in-store stylists, it really does seem like Jen is reliving her sorority days at Drake University, the midwestern school where she studied design.

■ Taking the Next Leap

What you get is what you give. All the support and encouragement she received essentially became Jen's business model for 1154 LILL. Looking for a way to be creative—and having people support her in that—Jen went out and built a business that supports other people's creativity. How ironic. As a child, Jen dreamed of being an art teacher surrounded by art supplies. Now Jen is a sort of teacher, showing customers how to design their own purses. True to her original business model, she has about 20 handbag styles and a constantly changing line of fabrics. Prices range from $70 to $130. Running 1154 LILL is a long way from punching the clock to design office spaces, but in a roundabout way her office design job got her where she is now.

And life just keeps moving along. Jen and her husband, who is a Burger King franchisee, had their first child in 2004. By that time, Jen had built the business up to where her employees could run the day-to-day operations and she was comfortable letting them. Although she says she's still pretty hands-on, she works fewer weekends now that she has a toddler to chase around. And as Jen's family grows, so does 1154 LILL.

After her expansion to Boston and Kansas City, Jen went back to her roots and started building a network of home party reps. Mainly, they're old friends or people who know someone who works at a LILL store. She calls that part of her business Local LILL and sees it as a way to expand without opening up more stores right away. The home party network is also a kind of market research: if demand starts to swell in certain areas, it could be a good place to open her next store. For now, Jen isn't talking about opening new stores; what she does want is for LILL to be the first brand people think of when they think custom-made handbags.

Thanks to supportive friends, bosses, and family, Jen made a business out of supporting other people's creativity. She has found her groove.

■ Chapter Eighteen

Kimberly Wilson, Founder of **Tranquil Space** and **TranquiliT** ■

Live Your Own Brand

Most people take up yoga to work off the tension of their jobs. Kimberly Wilson, 33, did it backward; she made her tension reliever into a job. In just a few years, she went from a promising career as a paralegal to launching her own brand, complete with the Tranquil Space yoga studio, TranquiliT clothing line, a Web site, hip yoga parties, and even a book club.

Kimberly's journey from a paralegal job at a top Washington, D.C. law firm to creating her Tranquil Space yoga studio and merchandise line shows the power of creating a brand based on your lifestyle. According to *Yoga Journal,* 15 million Americans do yoga, spending $27 billion annually on yoga products and classes. That's a lot of deep breathing. More than that, yoga isn't just about exercise: it reflects a desire for a creative outlet that is rampant in our society. Kimberly tapped into that trend and offers far more than just yoga classes. Her studio offers yoga-inspired clothing, book discussion groups, classes about managing money, and trunk shows to exhibit her designs and the creative fruits of other women's labors. Tranquil Space has become a unique, exceptional brand.

Before she took up yoga, Kimberly thought of her legal career as a sort of consolation prize. Kimberly had always thought she would become a psychotherapist, but when she didn't get into her graduate school of choice, she dropped that dream and took a paralegal course instead. All day long she would research and write clients' applications for trademarks, which would then be checked and approved by an attorney. Some of her clients were interesting, such as Cirque du Soleil, but the work wasn't inspiring. Kimberly was leading a double life: researching trademarks at her desk all day and considering law school, and then escaping during lunch hour into self-help books to help her get in touch with her inner creativity.

As she thought about what to do next, Kimberly took a yoga class on a whim, in part because of her reading of self-help books. The books advised her to uncover her creative self by changing her daily routine. So she did little things like taking a new way to work, cooking with a new herb, or listening to new types of music. Yoga turned out to be more than a whim.

"In any moment of decision," President Theodore Roosevelt said, "the best thing you can do is the right thing. The worst thing you can do is nothing." Kimberly knew she had to make a decision about her career, so she boldly took action and stepped into an entrepreneurial role. "I decided a law career just wasn't for me," she recalls. "I felt more passion for yoga and for building a community."

She started out small, making sure that she didn't overextend herself with excess overhead. To become certified to teach, she took numerous training courses around the country. Then she set up shop in her living room, where she had few expenses. And she didn't quit her day job until she saw that people in her D.C. neighborhood would come to her and pay to take classes.

Early on, some of the decisions that Kimberly made set the stage for her success. Those first flyers that Kimberly designed and photocopied are an example. Kimberly had always been the type to pay attention to detail; as a kid she would even rearrange the Wal-Mart toy aisle. So her flyers had a certain flair with details like a cartoon sketch of a woman gracefully standing in Tree Pose. It was eye-catching, and it got the attention of women who were looking for something different.

Another detail was the way Kimberly served tea and cookies to the class after they finished their yoga poses. It was an impulse she had when she first started out teaching in her home: it just seemed natural to serve refreshments to her guests. After she moved classes out of her home, Kimberly held onto the homey touch. While many yoga studios reflect the austere lifestyle traditionally followed by yogis in India, Kimberly's studio maintains an image of yoga that is fun, fashionable, and friendly.

That's what yoga is for Kimberly—a way to find like-minded friends and have fun. When she first moved to the D.C. area, she didn't know anyone. Even after studying there and working at a law firm, the rush of big-city life seemed to stand in the way of forming a tight group of friends like she'd had growing up in Oklahoma. Teaching yoga classes, she found the community she'd hungered for.

■ Starting from Scratch

For a while, Kimberly thought she might do things halfway, keeping her day job and practicing yoga on the side. She worked out a compromise by teaching yoga in her living room and at local gyms after work each day. There weren't many yoga studios around at the time as yoga was still new to conservative D.C. During class, she walked around gently explaining postures and breathing techniques to her students. After class, she served tea and cookies and chatted with her friends and the people they had brought to class. Kimberly felt like she'd found her niche.

That little group of friends in her living room told more friends, and soon she needed more space. So she graduated from her living room to a rented space in a nearby church and posted handmade flyers advertising her classes. In the first few months, Kimberly had so many students she couldn't teach them all herself, so she grew her operation by training teachers. After a year and a half teaching at the rented church space, she had eight teachers working for her. The operation grew from 12 students a week to more than 250. "We were bursting at the seams," Kimberly recalls.

"Learning to shrug is the beginning of wisdom." That's one of the aphorisms in *Simple Abundance,* a book that Kimberly read when she was searching for a fulfilling career. So Kimberly shrugged. Teaching yoga might seem an unlikely path, but she would try it anyway. She saw yoga as an extension of her teenage dream of becoming a psychotherapist, except now she was helping people discover their inner selves through exercise.

■ Underestimating Obstacles

Kimberly's first obstacle was that she never pictured herself as an entrepreneur. Growing up in Lawton, Oklahoma, she'd never seen skyscrapers until her family took a trip to San Francisco when she was in the ninth grade. She wondered, "What do all these people do in these big buildings?" But Kimberly *did* see herself as a mover and shaker. All through high school and college, she'd worked part-time and done active volunteer work on top of taking a full course schedule and staffing a crisis line.

When Kimberly started doing yoga and reading self-help books, she realized that maybe her skills did translate into entrepreneurship. "A lot of business is organizing," she figured, and that was something she was good at.

For the things she didn't feel confident about, such as financial planning, Kimberly paid an accountant. She also paid an attorney to help her draw up her business documents correctly and trademark her Tranquil Space and TranquiliT boutique brand.

The biggest struggle was managing other people and delegating. That's understandable, considering that in Kimberly's first business model she was doing all the teaching herself. Even when she hired teachers and added a Web site, she still put in long days running things by herself. The book that got her out of this rut,

Michael Gerber's *E-Myth,* gave her the advice to build a business, not a job.

Very soon, Kimberly realized that she should hire other people to run the day-to-day operations so that she could work on new projects and envision the future. Kimberly stayed away from a five-year plan because she wanted to remain flexible and awake to opportunities that came along. She still takes that approach.

One of her biggest challenges was a situation with her assistant, whom Kimberly had just promoted to the highest salary she'd ever paid anyone. Kimberly found out the assistant was using the studio's computer to post mean-spirited, personal attacks on Kimberly on her blog during work hours. She fired her the next day. "I was very disappointed; it was so emotional," Kimberly recalls. She also ended up having to do a lot of work herself until she found a replacement.

Another setback was a threat to her brand. A few teachers who had gone through her studio's training opened up their own studios nearby. To prevent brand dilution, Kimberly made an unpopular but important decision: she made her teachers sign an exclusivity and noncompete agreement. "That was a really tough decision, but I didn't need Tranquil Space IIs down the road that I didn't have quality control over and was not profiting from," she says. "You need to do what is in the best interest of your business."

■ Building Momentum

Since her first classes, Kimberly's business has continued to grow through word of mouth, but the market has changed since she first began teaching in her living room in 1999. Yoga classes are now everywhere, and yoga is a craze. In D.C., even Sandra Day O'Connor reportedly took yoga classes at the Supreme Court every Tuesday. There's even talk of a national yoga chain that plans to dominate the markets of major cities. And 75 percent of all gyms now offer some kind of yoga classes. Worse yet, she faces competition from one of her own trainees. But Kimberly's 1,800-square-foot yoga studio, which she opened in 2003, is thriving.

That's because Kimberly's brand leverages yoga to leapfrog into other markets. Her yoga studio feeds interest in her merchandise line, which drives sales into her Web site. Having such a strong brand has set her apart in the crowded yoga field. When yoga studios started coming out of the woodwork, she didn't lose market share. Women in D.C. think of Tranquil Space as a community center that feeds their creative journeys. This strong brand opens the door to many other business opportunities beyond classes.

While many business gurus have talked about the importance of planning and vision, Kimberly's brand grew organically in small steps. It started when students wanted something more to do after yoga classes, so Kimberly added additional workshops and community offerings such as a book club. "It just seemed right to offer more than just yoga," she says. Whenever teachers and students express an interest or offer to start up something, Kimberly sees it as a way to strengthen her brand and keep her studio in use. Some of the activities don't even build revenue—the book group takes a small donation for a local charity—but they offer people an additional reason to come to Kimberly's studio. If Kimberly had had a rigid plan in the beginning, she might not have taken advantage of all the opportunities along the way.

While not all of her studio's extracurricular activities increase revenue, her boutique and trunk shows do. Her boutique, for instance, features her own line of clothing. At first, the trunk shows featured only her line of yoga togs. Then the trunk shows evolved into mini trade shows featuring jewelry, soaps, and other products made by local women. These shows are also memorable events, with plenty of details like yoga demos, music, wine, and fun. It has built her a loyal following.

"We're tried and true, and people see us as a community," Kimberly says. "That means a lot to me."

■ Taking the Next Leap

Kimberly isn't a numbers person. She focuses on keeping her business profitable, serving her customers, and coming up with new ideas. This past year she saw her labors bear fruit in a growing bottom line. When her accountant looked at her numbers, Kimberly was a little shocked at how well she'd done: "I grossed a half a million dollars. How did that happen?"

It's really not a mystery. Kimberly took baby steps and little by little extended her brand over several revenue streams. Her brand includes yoga classes as well as superhip yoga-themed fashion events and online clothing sales. Kimberly builds this brand with her strengths: fussing over details, honing in on what her mostly female clientele wants, polishing the look of her studio and Web site, and staying open to new ideas and opportunities. And she pays experts to handle the legal and financial details that she's not so good at.

Building abundance this way feels effortless to Kimberly because she's doing what she loves. For her, yoga is something she does to feel good, and it's a means to launching a line of products and classes that serve women like her.

In 2005, she went to New York for her first trade show, presenting her TranquiliT line to the public. Maybe it will lead to more trunk shows at other boutiques or yoga studios. She's also writing a book. She could follow that with a nationwide book tour, sharing her story with others and encouraging them to leave their passionless jobs and do their own thing. Maybe she'll launch a boutique—independent of her studio—to sell her clothing line. She feels full of possibilities.

It all started out as a feeling of being unfulfilled, of wanting more than what a legal career could offer. And it turned into a brand that Kimberly finds almost effortless to build because it's all about serving women just like her.

Kimberly is living her brand.

▪ Chapter Nineteen

Willa Levin, Franchisee of **The UPS Store**

Patience

This story really hits home with me. My wife is a nurse, so over the years I've gotten to know dozens of her friends and hear the universal complaints about the nursing industry—which, by the way, has the highest burnout rate of any profession. Nurses are overworked, underpaid, spit on, shit on, and underappreciated. To become a nurse you have to be smart, dedicated, and ready to work. To stay a nurse, you have to be an angel of mercy!

I hope that every nurse in the country reads this story so that they can see a light at the end of the tunnel. Willa Levin's story proves that there is light, even if the tunnel may take years to dig. Her experience proves that there's a lot to be said for patience.

While many people in this book leaped into the excitement of building their own business, Willa took a more cautious route. She's proof that you don't have to have a new, unconventional approach to business models, the confidence to finesse business deals, or even a burning desire to achieve balance. For people like Willa, patience and caution enabled her to learn about business and make solid, smart choices. Her patience also comes in handy when dealing with demanding, hurried customers at her prosperous UPS Store franchises.

Like most of the people in this book, Willa worked her way to success by using her strengths. In her case, her strength was a steady, methodical approach to work that began in childhood when she overcame a pretty big obstacle: she didn't know how to speak English. Because Willa's parents had immigrated to Canada from the Netherlands before she was born and spoke only Dutch at home, her first day of school was a shock. "At first, it was really hard to understand what was going on," she recalls. "I just remember thinking, I have to do this." So she sat down with her mother every night and they learned the new language together. By the end of the year, Willa was at the top of her class.

She credits her parents for her entrepreneurial spirit. Leaving your native country, after all, is a pretty gutsy thing to do. With farmland scarce in their homeland, Willa's parents were driven by their desire to build something of their own. Working on the family's farm side by side with her father—milking cows, baling hay, and doing whatever else needed to be done—built Willa's patient nature.

Some people, like Susan at Barefoot Café or David Yorke from Barking Hound Village, have the resilience to pick themselves up when they get knocked down. Willa has the knack for avoiding the pitfalls that knock people down in the first place. For instance, on the farm she was calm and patient with the family's livestock and proudly points out that she was never once kicked by a cow. In business, she does her research and has always avoided bad contracts.

As a young adult, Willa's slow, steady approach to life led her to study nursing: she knew she would always have a job. She liked helping people, putting them at ease, and liked working hard. Right out of school, Willa found a job at Henry Ford Hospital, a large teaching hospital in downtown Detroit. "I wanted to be where the action was," she says. The next few years were a flurry of work. Since registered nurses were in demand, Willa was put in charge of a whole unit after just a few months. She rose to the challenge.

After a few years, she was looking for more challenges and became a personnel recruiter for Sinai Hospital. The job was exciting, with plenty of travel to colleges and job fairs where she looked for good nurses to hire for the hospital. It was then that she developed an uncanny sense for spotting a good employee: "After a while, you just know when you've found a good nurse." This is another entrepreneurial skill for the future.

Finally, in her tenth year as a nurse, Willa made a job move that finally pushed her down the path of entrepreneurship: she took a big increase in responsibility that came with a paltry raise. Willa became a head nurse, or nurse manager, on an oncology unit. There, she was in charge of staffing the whole unit. She ran 5 AM staff meetings and filled in for staff in emergencies. It was tough work with grueling 50-hour-plus weeks. "It just took over my life," she says. "My life was controlled 24 hours a day, seven days a week."

People—even patient people—burn out in demanding jobs. A fisherman will sit in his boat all day long and have the time of his life even if he doesn't catch one fish, as long as he thinks a great fish might come along any minute. Willa realized that there weren't any more fish in her lake. She'd nearly reached the end of her career path and suddenly had to face the harsh reality that she had reached the top of her field. At that point, things didn't look so rosy.

■ Starting from Scratch

Luckily, there was a bright spot. At lunchtime, Willa and another nurse manager, Leah, would meet in the cafeteria and plot their next career moves. Sitting down to their hurried lunches, the two nurses would come up with ideas for their own businesses. At first they figured they would do something related to nursing, maybe medical consulting or nurse staffing. After a couple of years of fantasizing, Willa and Leah took the first of many small steps: they registered for a ten-week small business class offered by Michigan State University.

That's where Willa and Leah realized they fit the profile of successful franchise operators. They wanted to work for themselves but didn't have a specific idea for a business. I run into this scenario all the time with my friends, family, colleagues, and clients. Picking from a list of franchises can be an extraordinary way to figure out a way to work on your own business. Plus they didn't want to do something risky. Already in their 30s, they didn't feel like jumping into an unproven business. And they'd learned some frightening statistics: 90 percent of small businesses fail within the first three years. Even though it meant paying 6 percent of their profits to a franchiser, the two nurses liked the safety of buying a proven business model.

Over the next nine months, Willa and Leah spent their spare time reading everything they could find about franchises. They learned that they should pick a mature franchise, one where the franchisees have a good success rate. At one point, they thought about a beauty supply franchise. Then one day, Leah noticed a Mailboxes Etc. for sale near her Grosse Point home. They looked up statistics, talked to the area franchisee, and interviewed other Mailboxes Etc. storeowners. They also looked into why the franchisee was selling; it turned out he just didn't have the patience to work with the public. Since Willa and Leah had long years of working with the public in their nursing jobs, they figured this wouldn't be a problem for them.

When it came to finding money for their business, they were creative. The asking price for the Mailboxes Etc. store was $130,000, so the two nurses financed most of the deal with a personal loan from the franchisee who was selling the store. Willa remembers that on the day they signed the loan papers and sale agreement, she felt she was "signing her life away." There she was, in her mid-30s, making a huge career change and taking on a big chunk of debt. But deep inside, she knew she and Leah could make it work.

They came up with a schedule for the first nine months. First, they would both keep part-time nursing jobs to build up their working capital. With meeting payroll and making loan payments, they wanted to build up a few months' cushion in case they had a slow month. Again, they were cautious, hardworking, and patient. Their style was not as flashy as some of the entrepreneurs that make headlines in the business press, but their approach worked for them.

More than anything, Willa and Leah were patient with each other and could offset each other's weaknesses. Willa, for example, says she tends to be the one to think more generally and come up with a vision for the future. Leah is more detail oriented. Both are great at customer service. "A good partner makes it work," Willa explains, "because the other person cares about the place as much as you do. So you can take time away and know that business is well taken care of."

Even with their great partnership and solid business plan, they didn't have smooth sailing. Like most people who start their own businesses, there's no way to avoid making a few mistakes or having just plain bad luck.

■ Underestimating Obstacles

To this day, Willa remembers that what scared her the most in those early years was a statistic she heard in her business class: only 10 percent of small businesses succeed beyond the first few years. The instructor countered that statistic with another: 90 percent of franchises succeed beyond their first years. The professor then provided the caveat that no business is foolproof.

Now, this isn't to say that franchises are for everyone. But for Willa and Leah, the safety of a franchise business model enabled them to take the leap into entrepreneurship that they probably wouldn't have done otherwise.

In the beginning, the hardest part about running the store was dividing their time between their other jobs. In the evenings, Willa would go to her midnight supervisor job, then rush home to catch a little sleep before heading to the store to relieve Leah, who was off to her afternoon job as a part-time staff nurse. This went on for the better part of their first year.

When you buy a franchise, it's not realistic to expect to make a profit to live off of in the first year; it usually takes two years. For one thing, there's the business loan to pay off. For another thing, the franchise takes a 6 percent cut of profits—which has to be paid on schedule. Nowadays, Willa estimates you'd have to take in about $400,000 gross sales a year to make a good living at a franchise store. But Willa and Leah weren't bothered by this and patiently worked their other jobs until they had built up their store to a level that allowed them to quit their jobs. To this day, they say that building up a cash reserve was one of the big reasons they succeeded.

One of the big draws of franchising is that an owner can build up to owning several stores and run a profitable little empire. With this in mind, Willa and Leah rushed into buying a second store as soon as they could. It was one of the few decisions they made without patiently weighing all the facts—and it turned out to be a mistake.

It happened two years after buying their first store. They heard of another Mailboxes Etc. store that was for sale and bought it. What they didn't look into was why the owner was selling; it turned out the location was a dog. It was in a low-traffic mall and was breaking even or generating a small profit—but nothing like the cash flow of their first store. Even when they stepped up advertising, which cut into profits, the store's traffic didn't improve much. "It didn't make sense to own a store where we had to expend so much energy to make so much less money," Willa says. They held onto the store for four years and then sold it to someone else who was willing to give it a try.

That taught them to stick with their strength, which was to patiently research each step before moving ahead. As Willa says: "Just because you've got a great name on your storefront, you can't assume that everything is going to be hunky dory."

■ Building Momentum

One of the things Willa liked about Mailboxes Etc., which was bought out by The UPS Stores in 2001, was that the franchise provided a great deal of advertising. Still, Willa and Leah learned that there's nothing like good old-fashioned word of mouth to bring in new customers. Sure, they cover their bases by sending out postcards, running newspaper ads, and buying inserts for local coupon mailings. But their best advertising comes from the small businesses that use their stores as a "first office."

Willa and Leah love working with these small, early-stage businesses that make up the bulk of their customers. They remember one man in particular, who was running an eBay store and had to get 20 packages out the door each day just to survive. They got to know him by his first name and looked forward to his visits each day. Willa knows how important it is for those little start-ups to know they can count on efficient, dependable service to keep them organized. Plus, with the partners' experience running nursing staffs, they're good at inspiring their employees to give great service.

Another way the partners drive business is by picking great locations. Their first store, which they still own, has 60,000 cars pass by every day. "A good owner can make a bad location okay," Willa says, "but you'll never make it great. With a good location, a good owner can really go to town."

Above all—even with great locations and great service—the price needs to be right. Willa learned her pricing strategy long ago from her area franchisee: "You'll go out of business faster by marking it up too little than by marking it up too much." In other words, to have a successful business you have to have the right margins in place. (And once your brand is associated with low prices, it's hard to raise them, as Sara Blakely explained in Chapter 7.) It might sound like common sense, but amazingly, many owners are so afraid of upsetting customers that they don't charge enough to make a decent profit. Maybe that's because finding the price the market will bear doesn't mean that everyone will like it.

Willa remembers one angry woman who said their shipping prices were outrageous and then walked out and slammed the door. The woman even called back to report that she was able to ship her package for $1.50 less at the post office and insisted on knowing Willa's markup. Willa tried skirting the issue, but the irate lady demanded to know the percentage markup. When Willa bluntly refused, the woman cussed her out and said she hoped the store went out of business. Willa didn't take it to heart, because most customers realize they get what they pay for! So another lesson in business: If you're good, don't be afraid to charge for it.

When times get tough, Willa remembers the rewards of hard work. When she was a child, her parent's farm was prosperous but the work was often demanding. One of her proudest memories is the time she first helped her dad bring in hay. It happened when a farmhand was too sick to finish baling hay with Willa's father. She recalls him standing in the living room, distraught, saying, "What am I going to do?" It was too late to hire last-minute help, and the hay couldn't be left to rot. Even though she was only ten years old, Willa remembers begging him to let her help, knowing her father thought she was too young. "It was critical that it get done," Willa recalls. "And then I did it and it really helped out. I'll never forget that."

■ Taking the Next Leap

Willa and Leah took their professor's forecast of 90 percent failure and turned the odds around to 90 percent success. With all their planning and patient research, they've done well. First, all their research made them realize their first store had a great location with plenty of drive-by traffic and easy access. Second, their easygoing, calm-under-pressure personalities endeared them to the already-stressed-out customers who came to their store wanting something shipped in a hurry or needing to set up a mailbox rental on the fly. Third, they were shrewd about building up a cash reserve, even if it meant working two jobs at the start.

Seventeen years later, the former nurses own three stores, including their first, which recently ranked 64 out of 4,000 stores nationally. On average, their three stores each bring in about $500,000 a year in gross sales.

Not only do Willa and Leah earn a nice salary, they've also built a valuable asset. Many nurses and middle management types make somewhere around $50,000 or so a year. Most of those people, if you ask them, would rather work for themselves. They stay with their jobs because it gives them a feeling of security, but in reality they're not building long-term security. That's because the average person isn't saving enough for retirement. To retire with a modest income, you need to save more than $1 million. Most people are not able to do that working an average job. But an average franchise business can replace a mediocre wage and build an asset for retirement at the same time. Looking at it this way, why work for someone for $40,000 or $50,000 when you could self-finance a franchise, replace your wage, and build an asset you can call your own?

Willa and franchise owner Alan Thompson (Chapter 11) advise people who go the franchise route to take a patient, careful approach and ask a lot of questions. Go to specific franchises and talk to people who are in the business already. They both advise franchisees to buy into a mature franchise where the kinks have been worked out; however, as they point out, mature franchises usually charge higher start-up fees.

In the future, Willa and Leah aren't sure what their plans will be. For now, they're sitting tight with their three stores. They just acquired their third store two years ago, and it was their first out-of-the-box UPS Store; the others were already running under different owners. So far, that location has turned out to be excellent.

Sometimes Willa thinks about what would have happened if she hadn't dreamed about moving beyond her nursing career. She wouldn't have the retirement savings that she's been able to save from her franchise business, and she wouldn't have the freedom she's earned. More than anything, she enjoys her work more. "That's the biggest thing," Willa says. "Shipping is a fun business for us."

Having patience and finding a business partner with the same quality gives them both peace of mind. Each knows that whenever they leave the other in charge, the other partner will take care of things.

Willa and Leah have the patience to succeed.

■ Chapter Twenty

Achieve Balance

If I were a mother of three, I would want to be Jen Klair. Jen wanted it all: the adventure of business and the freedom to stay home and raise her young daughters. With her online children's boutique, JenKlairKids.com, now she really does have it all. Starting with a line of homemade blankets stitched by her mother, the site now offers a line of 1,200 luxury baby and children's items. After one of her blankets made the cover of *Better Homes and Gardens Kids Rooms,* orders started pouring in. Now Jen joins the growing ranks of "mompreneurs" running their own home-based businesses.

In the beginning, Jen Klair Kids really started off as a hobby. When a major competitor took Jen to court in her first year online, she realized she was onto something big.

Jen always knew she'd do something different, not corporate. Since she was a child, she'd always loved adventure. Growing up, her father's finance job moved the family all over the United States and even to London for a time. But her mother always stayed home—wherever it was—and made a stable base for Jen and her two brothers. Her father's high-powered career inspired Jen to be a risk taker, but she also wanted to be like her mother and stay home and raise kids. Somehow, she knew she would find a way to do both.

Moving around every two or three years, Jen's family led a fun sort of gypsy life, and she got a taste for different styles of dress and ways of doing things. Wherever she was, she always stuck out a little bit. And she didn't really mind that.

Following her gut feelings usually worked out well for Jen, even if it didn't earn her much money at first. After college, Jen and her husband-to-be sold their used cars and set out for St. Thomas for two months with the dream of writing books together. Who hasn't had a dream like that? I think we'd all like to go live on an island somewhere and effortlessly earn a living. But that's not reality. With no clear way to earn a living, it ended up being more of an extended vacation. They didn't write any books, but they did enjoy the French countryside feel of the Virgin Islands. And something else happened. Jen may not have known it at the time, but she was taking in the soft color scheme and subtle elegance of French country design. And she was learning to be a risk taker.

On their return, Jen did a four-year stint working in media relations for trade associations in Washington, D.C. It was as close as she got to the corporate world, and she didn't like it.

Eventually, they settled down and married and her husband took a teaching job. With his income for stability, Jen followed her instincts to start her first business: a pet-sitting service. In the Lake Tahoe community where they lived at the time, there were plenty of on-the-go folks with cherished pets. She visited homes and cared for animals, literally working day and night. With no employees to pay and hardly any overhead expenses, she made about $30,000 a year from the service. Combined with her husband's teaching income, the young couple was making enough for their needs, but they weren't able to put away much savings.

In 1998, Jen's life changed when she had their first child and relocated again. As the family settled into their Southern California home, Jen fell in love with gorgeous, high-end baby products and outfitted her daughter's room, at great cost as any new parent will tell you. By the time she was expecting their second daughter, Jen and her mother started shopping upholstery shops for fabrics to outfit the new baby's room using Jen's own designs. Blankets were their specialty—Jen's mother even taught herself to sew just so she could make the unusual designs that Jen thought up.

It became a hobby for the two of them to search upholstery shops for just the right luxury fabrics to make new blankets. The designs were unusual. One of Jen's favorites was toile, a tapestry-like fabric with French countryside scenes printed on it. She also had blankets made of vintage handkerchiefs, faux fur, and satin fabric. Not the kind of thing people normally find on baby blankets, but they looked incredibly exotic. And they were lined with soft cotton chenille, the kind of fabric that makes everyone think of their grandma's bedspread.

Maybe Jen and her mother were a little obsessed with baby blankets for a while, but they loved the look and feel of these handmade blankets, and they were having fun coming up with eye-catching designs. Best of all, the blankets stood out—and Jen had always liked standing out. These blankets were obviously one-of-a-kind, handmade heirlooms, not something off the shelf from Gymboree or Baby Gap. People would stop and look when she was out with her children at parks and restaurants and ask, "Wow, Jen, I really like your baby blanket. Where can I get one?"

One day, while Jen and her mother were looking at fabrics, Jen realized—this could be a business. She was learning the first lesson of the HUNT: harness what you have. First, she had great taste in baby items. Second, she had a fierce desire to work for herself and define her own work schedule. Some people might think working from home was a liability, but for Jen it was the beginning of a great business model.

■ Starting from Scratch

It was 2001 and Internet shopping was just hitting its stride. Sure, Amazon and large catalogs were doing well, but it wasn't common to have a small, online specialty store. Jen's entrepreneur-ial thinking—her desire to do things her way—told her that the In-ternet would give her the flexibility she needed to run a business from home. A virtual store would still be a lot of work, but she would be home. She was willing to take the risk.

Jen's idea became reality from the moment she picked up pen and paper and sketched out designs of how she wanted her Web site to look. Since she didn't have money for focus groups or con-sultants, she just went with what she liked: a warm, feminine color scheme; simple navigation buttons; and a catchy slogan, "A little bit of luxury for little ones." Jen had done a lot of shopping on the In-ternet, so she knew what kinds of sites she liked. Also, she found a Web designer (another stay-at-home mom) to create the actual site using Jen's sketches.

In the beginning, Jen kept things simple and kept overhead ex-penses low. At first, her site was hosted as a Yahoo! store, which set her up with a shopping cart, secure credit card ordering, and cus-tomer tracking for a small monthly fee. Nothing fancy, but it worked and later had the unexpected payoff of a Yahoo! forum. What little money she made in those early days went toward pay-ing her Web designer, paying the Web hosting fee, and buying baby items to sell on her site.

While her daughters napped, Jen would go online and log onto the Yahoo! forum for Internet e-tailers. She learned a lot from the other online stores. For instance, the concept of drop shipping: a customer could order a product from Jen's Web site and the whole-saler would send it directly to the customer, so the product would never have to go through Jen's warehouse. Good thing, because her warehouse was her home. And things were already bursting at the seams with boxes of baby blankets and designer diaper bags taking up every spare inch of her living space.

In that first year, Jen didn't follow a sophisticated business plan; she just used her common sense. She visited children's boutiques, Kids Expos, antiques fairs, and craft shows to find undiscovered de-signers who made baby bibs, clothing, and diaper bags. Whatever cash she took in from baby blanket orders she put back into buying product from these home crafters at wholesale prices. Sometimes, she sold the handmade goods on consignment.

When it came to picking out merchandise, Jen just stocked her site with things she and her friends liked—and she also talked to customers. Jen's daughters learned early that when mom had her "business voice" on the phone, she was working. During one of those phone conversations, a customer mentioned a line of organic cotton clothing that she liked. As soon as Jen got off the phone with her, she looked into the company and started carrying that line. Also, Jen set up her Web site so that customers can give suggestions during the checkout process. To this day, she gets lots of ideas from these hints.

Mostly, that first year was trial and error, Jen says. She always asked a lot of questions whenever she didn't understand something. Gradually, she and her mother came up with 15 different blanket designs, including safari and Hawaiian prints, and lacy pillowcase dresses. She knew her designs weren't for everyone, but Jen wasn't selling to everyone. She was selling to people who wanted something different and were willing to pay for it.

■ Underestimating Obstacles

In that first year, Jen likes to say that the best thing that happened to her was also the worst: she was sued by a competitor who accused her of copying her ideas. Now, most people would think of a lawsuit as a stressful and expensive nuisance. At the time, it was. But when it was over and Jen had settled the legal issues, a lightbulb lit up for her: "I had a great concept and business idea," she says. "And it was worth fighting for."

Ironically, it took a lawsuit for Jen to see that her business wasn't just a fun hobby to keep her busy and make a little money while she was home with the kids. The lawsuit made her realize that her competitor saw her as a threat and wanted to put her out of business. "It really just made me stronger and more determined to succeed," she says. It made Jen see that she'd built something valuable. "I look back on it now and realize that was the time that my company took on a new life, and we've been growing ever since."

But not everyone took Jen seriously in those early days. At first, she had a lot of doors slammed in her face. "Oh, you're *just* a Web site? Call us when you have a storefront," suppliers would say. But Jen was determined to have her business be Web-only, so she took these comments in stride.

Her days in media relations had taught her focus, discipline, and how to think on her feet. So when people made comments that an Internet-only company wasn't viable, she shot back statistics about how rapidly consumers were switching to Internet shopping. She was polite and professional, even when others weren't.

One way to gain respect in the retail world is to create some buzz about your product. You get people talking about how unusual or glamorous your product is. One of the best ways to do that is to make a splash in the print media. Somehow, glossy magazines make a product look more real. Jen knew she needed to find a way to get her blankets noticed and on the map. From her work in media relations, Jen figured her best bet would be to just keep sending photos of her merchandise to magazine editors in hopes that one day she would get some attention.

■ Building Momentum

Instead of sinking a lot of money into advertising, Jen spent her first year building up inventory and learning how to run an online business. To get the word out about her new Web site, she e-mailed friends and family, asking them to forward her store information to everyone they knew. She set up a booth at a local holiday craft show, where she displayed her blankets and some other baby products she'd started to sell. She even put flyers at her daughter's preschool. "I would do anything to get my name out there," Jen recalls.

After putting all that effort into getting customers, Jen wanted to keep her customers coming back. Young families need more than one blanket, she reasoned, and she wanted people to think of her whenever they needed a baby gift or something special for their own children. So she worked on getting customers to return. For every order that went out, she included a 10 percent discount coupon for that customer's next order. She also signed up customers to her mailing list and sent out an e-mail once a month with "new arrivals" and usually a coupon for their next purchase. To this day, return customers generate half her business, and she prides herself on generating loyalty to her brand.

Behind the scenes, Jen has other people who leverage her idea: her family. Her husband doesn't complain about the boxes taking up space in the guest room or the fact that dinner isn't usually ready on time. And her parents, especially her mother, have been a huge help. There must be an entrepreneurial gene in her family, because her two brothers also have their own businesses: one has his own law practice and the other his own restaurant.

Outside of her family and friends, Jen shamelessly courts magazine editors, sending them e-mails and product photos. Once she tried a paid search engine listing on Yahoo! It seemed like a pretty good way to drive interest during the holiday shopping season, but Jen wasn't convinced it was worthwhile. Instead of ads, her media relations background tells her to keep showcasing her products to magazine editors. It takes only a little effort to send regular e-mails each month.

In 2004, she finally got the media attention she craved. *Better Homes and Gardens Kids Rooms* featured one of her blankets on its cover. That year, revenue was up 60 percent. Sales continue to grow. Magazine photo editors now call her to get hard-to-find products they want to feature in magazine photos. *Pregnancy* magazine has featured her products a few times and so have a few other magazines. In 2005, Jen hired a publicist to keep drumming up interest at magazines—she figures the publicist's fee will more than pay for itself in brand recognition.

■ Taking the Next Leap

Meanwhile, as sales shot up, Jen's mother continued busily sewing all of Jen's signature baby blankets and pillowcase dresses. Incredibly, her mother kept up with demand. By mid-2005, Jen hired another seamstress because her mother was finally getting worn out with the increasing demand. Even with paid help, Jen and her mother want to keep close tabs on the blanket sewing because the blankets and pillowcase dresses are the site's bread and butter. Having all the work in-house, literally, makes for great quality control. So Jen is picky about the sewing.

There was another milestone in 2005 when Jen's mom made a little fabric roll for her grandchildren to tote around crayons. "Whenever I went to a restaurant or anywhere, I had crayons all over the place," Jen says. When she got things under control with the Color Caddy, "people were going crazy asking for it." Demand flew through the roof, and the Color Caddy became the first item that Jen sold wholesale to other retailers. It's also the only item she has had commercially manufactured. Maybe wholesaling will be another trend. As a good entrepreneur, Jen is going to wait and see what opportunities arise.

In the beginning, all Jen had was a great sense of style and a willingness to work hard. She could have rented a storefront and set up a children's store like a lot of women did in suburban Los Angeles or made a career of selling at craft shows. But Jen had always pictured herself working from home while raising her daughters, and long retail hours didn't suit her.

When people want something badly enough, they have a way of getting it. That's why starting a business that serves your personal needs, as well as your financial needs, is a winning formula.

In just four short years, Jen built her own Internet store and has a product that she's wholesaling. Plus she has something even more valuable: Jen has balance.

■ Chapter Twenty-One

Giovanni The Margarita King, Founder of **The Margarita King**

Tireless Energy

Giovanni The Margarita King is a fistful of dynamite. Maybe it's the way he stands at a towering 4 feet 11 inches, looks you in the eye, and shakes your hand like you're his best friend in the world. Or the way he insists that The Margarita King is his real name: sure, Gio... Trust me on this, Giovanni has a personality that will blow you away.

Gio didn't start out being The Margarita King. An Italian who grew up in Colombia, thanks to his father's job in the oil business, Gio studied to be an architect. When his mentor at the time told him there was no money to be made designing buildings, Gio was lured by the United States and its restaurant industry. He headed to San Francisco to try his hand at the restaurant business.

He started at the very bottom, as a busboy, getting his hands dirty cleaning tables. In just a year and a half, Gio worked his way up to host, waiter, bartender, kitchen manager, and finally restaurant manager. All along, he knew he was going to run his own show one day. Within two years of starting as a busboy, he begged, borrowed, and finagled just enough money to begin his own restaurant: Las Margaritas. "Borrow from everybody, but pay everyone back," he says.

At Las Margaritas, this little man put his huge personality to work. People started calling him The Margarita King for his awesome margaritas. When diners came in he would hug them, seat them himself, and treat them like his best friends. The Margarita King also made sure that every single person who worked for him did the same: "All my people work with energy," he says. "If you're not happy I don't need you." From the chefs to the busboys, Gio expected everyone to give their all and treat the customers like "a billion dollars." A billion is a lot in any currency, even in pesos.

Gio built and sold nine different Mexican restaurants in San Francisco over 15 years. Those margaritas eventually put Gio at the top of the San Francisco "Best Margarita" list. They were so good that he won seven years in a row for best margarita before they retired him and forced him to become a judge. I always thought that margaritas were from Mexico, and here we have an Italian dominating the competition. It's the equivalent of the Russians besting the United States in baseball; it just shouldn't happen.

Anyway, Gio couldn't help but wonder about the commercial viability of his margarita recipe. Then the lightbulb went on: Gio would bottle his margaritas and sell them ready-made in stores.

■ Starting from Scratch

The heart of any drink recipe worth its salt is the liquor. With margaritas, it's tequila. Now anyone who has been through their 21st birthday in a blur knows that the beautiful golden hue of tequila walks a fine line between the exquisite and the undrinkable. Made from the juices of the blue agave plant, families in Mexico have been guarding their harvesting and aging processes for centuries. If Gio was going to make world-class margaritas in a bottle, he needed to find tequila that was best of breed.

That's how Gio ended up on a golf course in Mexico, playing 18 holes with Raul Plascencia, liquor mogul and owner of Espolon Tequila. Espolon produced the finest tequila Gio had ever tasted. However, without jumping the gun, Gio will tell you that in order to develop a significant business relationship with anyone, "you need to feel the energy between you." In Mexico, finding that energy before doing a deal is a common way of doing business; in America, we call it listening to your gut. After getting to know Plascencia, Gio did feel the right vibe, and he had found the perfect golden hue for his baby "The Margarita King" in a bottle!

In the developmental stages of his new liquor venture, Gio woke up early, charged himself up with an hour of tai chi and meditation, and spent the day energetically hitting the phones to build the right network. Gio took on the task of putting together bottled margaritas just like he took on the task of opening his first restaurant. But instead of busing tables or serving food, he was learning about the tequila business step-by-step, making the perfect mix and perfect package for his new lusciously green cocktail.

After putting together a deal with Espolon for tequila, he moved on to the other steps: label design, printing, and finding suppliers for sugar cane, lime juice, and orange liqueur. It took nearly two years to line up suppliers and to navigate the regulations and permits of both Mexico and the United States. Inch-by-inch, Gio put together the many pieces of the bottled margarita deal. He built the margaritas from the bottom up, starting with the finest tequila, just as he did in his restaurants, always making sure he had the best chefs and waitstaff. As Gio says, "If you have a weak foundation, then the house will fall."

Then came the decision about how many bottles to produce. Friends advised him to start with 200 cases. "Don't spend your money on something that doesn't sell," they told him. But Gio knew better. "When you think more, you get more," he figured. "If you're going to play, play high." He invested half a million dollars on his first production run of 1,000 cases. People said he was crazy, but this 4-foot-11 giant knew he was just thinking big.

■ Underestimating Obstacles

With his 1,000 cases sitting in a warehouse, Gio went to the number one distributor in the country, Southern Wine and Spirits. This time, all his hope and energy for The Margarita King brand couldn't even get him past the front door. "Basically, they told me that it was too expensive." Unlike the competitors, Gio's ready-made margaritas used top-shelf liquor.

With the number one player saying no, Gio decided to speak with one of the more regional players, Young's Market Co., which did most of its business in his home state of California. He sat down with the Young's Market people and tried a slightly different approach. He said, "Let's drink first and talk later. If you don't all love the drink, then there is no meeting!" Well, it turns out they loved the drink, and after an hour and a half of taste testing, the executive team loved it even more. However, as the revelry subsided, the discussion turned to price.

"The room got so quiet, it was like somebody had died," Gio recalls. "Gio, we love you but we don't know if you've done your homework," they told him. With the competitor's brand selling for $12.95, they wanted to know how he was going to put his bottle next to theirs and sell it for $19? The meeting ended, and Young's Market promptly told Giovanni that it would revisit the whole deal if he could get 20 or 30 local stores to sell his pricey bottled margaritas. "Okay, no problem, someday you guys will see me here again," Gio told them and walked out.

"I went through a nightmare," Gio recalls. He figured he would sell his Margarita King bottles even if he had to sell them out of the trunk of his car. And that's just what he did. Storing his 1,000 cases in a warehouse, Gio spent six months going through a mountain of paperwork to get his distributor's license. Then he set off with his fiancée Gigi and hit the pavement. "Me and Gigi would load up ten cases in my car and go out from 7:00 in the morning until 11:00 at night, going store to store, knocking on doors and introducing ourselves, and telling them about The Margarita King." After four

months, they had 150 accounts—well beyond the 30 that the Young's
Market folks had asked for. That's just how Gio does it—big!

■ Building Momentum

Gio knew that before he went back to the big distributors, he
needed to create demand for his bottled margaritas.

It made him think back to his restaurant days when he took
over the enormous Barcelona, which was $1.2 million in debt.
That's a lot of debt. Most restaurants don't even gross $1.2 million
in a year. But Giovanni saw potential, even though a normal night
consisted of bad Spanish music, scores of empty seats, and watery
margaritas. A week into the turnaround, he got a phone call for a
ten-seat reservation. He looked over the empty floor and said,
"Sorry sir, we are full tonight. You are going to have to call at least a
week in advance for a reservation like that."

His fiancée, Gigi, thought he was crazy. "Giovanni, what are
you doing? We have no one here and this place is sinking like the
Spanish armada!" Relax, he told everyone. "We need to create a demand; if we create it they will come." Thanks to a turnaround in the
kitchen, his famous margaritas, and Gio's energetic spoiling of the
customer, the ship did turn around. Pretty soon there was a two-
hour wait every night and a two-week waiting list for reservations.

Gio was going to do the same thing for his Margarita King brand.
One hundred and fifty accounts were enough to get him a distributor deal, but after his initial frustrations he knew he needed to score
big. So he hired a sales director to rack up more accounts to sell his
bottled margaritas in stores. After eight months, they had a total of
750 stores and restaurants selling The Margarita King. "We were all
basically hawking cases out of our trunks," Gio remembers.

One of the biggest victories was landing the account for Beverages and More, California's largest liquor store chain. Month after
month, Gio couldn't even get an appointment with the head honcho.
Finally, Gio just showed up at the division head's office. "How many

times do I have to tell you, I don't have time for you now?" the guy
said. But Gio stood firm and left him a bottle: "I want you to taste it;
if you don't like it call me and tell me to just get the hell out of here."
Five minutes later, as Gio is driving away, his cell phone rang. "The
guy says, 'This the best margarita I ever tasted!' And I said, 'Oh my
God, this is the best news I ever heard in my life.'"

Then there was another hurdle. The Beverage and More folks
wanted to know the name of his distributor because they didn't
deal with bottlers. That's when Gio, the one-product distributor,
turned on the charm. He swore to fill all the orders they needed for
all their stores. "If I fail once, kick me out," he said. "You'll have the
best service you ever had in your life." He got the account.

■ Taking the Next Leap

After pounding the pavement for a year to get things going, Gio
finally scored a meeting with the country's biggest distributor—the
people who wouldn't even talk to him a year before.

Then Gio did a shrewd thing. He remembered his restaurant
lessons about creating demand. He called back the Young's Market
folks, the smaller distributor that met with him and loved his margaritas but couldn't swallow his asking price. After all, he did tell
them he'd be back one day. And he had a feeling that he would be
treated better at a smaller distributor. Young's Market asked him to
come back and sealed an agreement—and Gio canceled the meeting
with the larger competitor. That's the kind of negotiator he is.

When Gio does anything, he puts all his energy into it—even
when other people laugh and tell him he's crazy. Once, when one of
his restaurants couldn't pull in a Sunday brunch crowd, he got a
bunch of high school cheerleaders to wave in traffic off the street!
Genius—I'm sure I would have stopped! He also knows when to
stop. His last restaurant, the Barcelona, was going full speed ahead
when the landlord tripled the rent. There was no way his business

could absorb that, so he threw in the towel and concentrated on his bottled margaritas.

With The Margarita King brand, Gio is still shooting for the stars. He expects to see sales of about 100,000 cases in 2005. But he won't be content until he reaches one million cases. "You will see that very soon," he says. At that rate, he would be doing about $140 million in revenue, which would make his company worth about $1.8 billion.

And he's thinking even bigger. Now that he has an operations manager and a great team of folks working for him, Gio's next dream is to build a tequila distillery in Mexico.

Whatever business he's in, Gio's secret is his tireless energy: "When you do anything, make sure you put all your energy into it, and always use the best tequila."

Conclusion

The 21 very different industries and entrepreneurs profiled here are meant to inspire you, showing you how this group of ordinary people built flourishing businesses by starting with their talents and social networks. Some industries may speak to you, others might not. Even if you can't see yourself in a particular industry, its secrets are universal.

Just like you, most of the entrepreneurs in this book didn't just throw everything down to become an entrepreneur. There are no rules when it comes to entrepreneurship. Some people, like Alan Thompson, can tolerate a lot of risk and even the stress of bankruptcy, but most of us would choose to be more cautious. Take, for instance, Willa Levin, who worked as a nurse for 15 years before buying a franchise in her late 30s. While the folks who risk everything get a lot of attention, most of us can pick a safer route while using the principles of the HUNT.

One of the common themes that I want to reiterate is the power of the media. You don't have to be famous to be featured in a national magazine; Maria Churchill was nowhere near famous and yet her shoe Web site was featured in ten fashion magazines in one year.

In their own way, every single one of my subjects paid keen attention to projecting their businesses over radio, TV, and the Internet.

Using the power of the media doesn't necessarily mean buying expensive ads; the best advertising costs nearly nothing. For instance, collecting e-mail addresses from customers and sending a daily or weekly e-mail is virtually free; a Web site is inexpensive; and attracting magazine and TV attention is priceless. Many entrepreneurs told me that they targeted national magazine editors—or celebrities like Oprah—and courted them with regular e-mail contacts about their business. It may take time, but that's how Jen Klair got her baby blanket on the cover of a decorating magazine, a move that rocketed her sales.

If you do pay for advertising, make sure it's worth every dollar you spend. Consider something attention getting and outrageous, like Jon Shibley's radio ads ("The biggest no-brainer in the history of the world") and Matt Lindner's print ads ("Thank God for CANS!"), or Steve Bercu's bumper stickers ("Keep Austin Weird"), which he gives away free to customers. However you do it, paid advertising may have its place in your business model—just be sure to use the media that gives you the most bang for your buck. Bottom line, even in this day and age people still fail to see the power of a quality Web site. Don't make that mistake.

I'd like to emphasize, too, how important it is to seek out a positive role model, no matter what stage of your career. For years I have thought that we live in a world that lacks positive role models. The media are filled with stories about corporate scandals, violent crimes, war, and corrupt politicians. Even some of our favorite professional athletes have gone down the path of impropriety, steroid use, and high-profile crime. We're living in an age when it's harder than ever for our children, our peers, and even our parents to find people to look up to. Just because good mentors are hard to find doesn't mean they can't be found. So take time to seek them out.

My deep desire, and a major reason I set out to write this book, is to find these role models—for you and for me: ordinary people that we can all relate to, normal people like you and me who didn't start out with a whole lot. They all started from scratch. At one point or another, they all created something from the ground up. Some of them had a burning desire to make the entrepreneurial leap, while others were forced into it after losing their jobs. Hopefully, this will help you choose to make the leap instead of being forced to make the leap.

Mastering the art of the HUNT is a universal strategy for entrepreneurial success. The 21 secrets can in some way help each and every one of us. And the people I interviewed, now friends from all the time we spent together, are meant to lead you in the right direction—perhaps a new direction—just as a great leader and mentor should.

Hopefully, while you're reading this you've already gotten some ideas. Chances are, the stories in this book will make you realize something about yourself. If not, go back over Part One and think about harnessing what you have. Maybe you have a hobby that you love or a cause that you can turn into a business. If you're the insightful type, like Ian Gerard, maybe you can see undiscovered, everyday wisdom that most people would like to be a part of. If you need confidence, start small and try something that you know will work, like Dave Helfrich and his one-day sunglasses sale.

How can you actually make one of these businesses happen? Take a good look at the nuts and bolts of each story and the practical steps of how each entrepreneur got the ball rolling. Sara Blakely drove to North Carolina to get her prototype made; Giovanni went door-to-door selling his bottled margaritas from his car trunk; Jen Klair paid a friend to design her Web site; and Warren Brown had a cake party to get his first orders.

You can also modify these business plans and make them your own. Let's say, like Dany Levy, you have a passion for writing and have the creativity to come up with something new and interesting each day. Who's to say you couldn't do the exact same thing about a topic you love, like sports, politics, or even lawn care? To be economically viable, you could have a fraction of *DailyCandy*'s million subscribers—many magazines have far south of 100,000 subscribers. The idea is to take your own creativity and transform one of these business models into your own.

On a final note, I asked my entrepreneurs to give me their five best tips for success in business, which can be found on my Web site: *http://www.wesmoss.com.* I thought I would get very different tips from every single person. Instead, there was remarkable similarity and numerous parallels from list to list. Nearly every entrepreneur spoke about operating in an industry that they love (*H*). They also talked about reacting to obstacles by being flexible and adapting to market changes (*U*). Another important theme was involving the right people: hiring those who complement and support you, interacting in your local community, and having trusted advisors (*N*). Most important, each entrepreneur advises not just recognizing an opportunity but taking steps to capitalize on an opportunity (*T*).

Every person in this book recognized and took advantage of a need in the market, whether it was for dinner delivery, up-to-date fashion news, women's underwear, affordable art, bottled margaritas, baby blankets, designer shoes, or doggie day care. They all moved forward and did something about it. They did and so can you.

If you can see yourself doing something new, or something you read about in this book, try it. You owe it to yourself.

Happy hunting, and let me know how it goes.